1968

# ROBERT BROWNING'S MORAL-AESTHETIC THEORY

## 1833–1855

# Robert Browning's
# Moral-Aesthetic Theory
## 1833–1855

*by*

Thomas J. Collins

UNIVERSITY OF NEBRASKA PRESS · LINCOLN

The material in Chapter I first appeared in different form
in " Shelley and God in Browning's *Pauline: Unresolved
Problems," Victorian Poetry*, III (Summer 1965), 151–160.

*Publishers on the Plains*

UNP

Manufactured in the United States of America

To my wife Jeannette,
and Mark, Kristen and
Brendan, our children

# Contents

# Introduction

This study is an attempt to present a unified and coherent analysis of the progressive development of Robert Browning's ideas concerning the nature and purpose of art, and the role of the artist, between 1833 and 1855. It is generally recognized that the growth of Browning's aesthetic is closely related to, and in large part dependent on, the growth of his moral ideas, that is, on his conception of man and of man's relationship to society and to God. It is also generally recognized that by 1855 Browning had clearly formulated his theory of imperfection—that the artist, and indeed all men, must pursue the infinite, even though it is unattainable, and that this pursuit must be attempted recognizing, and to some degree celebrating, the always incomplete and ultimately disappointing nature of the finite. However, despite the proliferation of Browning studies in the last decade, there is as yet no single work which examines, through a detailed chronological study of his early poetry, the progress of Browning's movement toward the goal he finally did reach in 1855.

This work does not pretend to present a new view of Browning's development, and it does not promise its reader an original philosophic theory concerning the end result of that development. But it is intended to supply, particularly for the needs of the student of Victorian literature, what has hitherto been lacking in Browning studies: a careful step-by-step analysis of the development of Browning's moral-aesthetic ideas—the problems he faced, the solutions he formulated as he grew toward his poetic maturity—and an examination of the intimate connection which exists between that mature work and the apprentice work out of which it evolved.

The justification of this kind of study lies within its limitations.

There are in print a number of excellent essays which concentrate on the explication of Browning's individual poems, and there are also numerous critical works on Browning which attempt to support a thesis by citing passages divorced from their poetic context. However, there is, to the best of my knowledge, no full-length examination which attempts to set forth an interpretative reading of Browning's poetry up to 1855 by depending primarily on a close adherence to the poetic texts, and by analyzing the texts, not in terms of the detachable, fragmentary, and isolated statements they might contain, but in terms of the relationship of such statements to the individual poems in which they occur, as well as the continuous thematic relationships which bind one poem to another.

Such a study will, I think, be beneficial to students undertaking a serious study of Browning, and to teachers of Victorian literature who have not had the opportunity to work painstakingly through the important, but difficult, early stages of Browning's poetic career. It is to be hoped that this book will also prove useful to others who are interested in what a major nineteenth-century English poet thought about the nature of poetry, and about the function of the poet and his poetry in society.

Although the focus of the following study is limited to Browning's poetry, and the development of Browning's ideas within the context of that poetry, the student of Victorian literature should bear in mind that there is a larger, and extremely important, context within which Browning himself must be seen: the cultural context—the intellectual and social milieu of the nineteenth century. A brief reading list is included in the bibliography to assist the student in his study of the Victorian cultural and social framework.

# ROBERT BROWNING'S MORAL-AESTHETIC THEORY
## 1833–1855

## CHAPTER ONE

# *Pauline* and the Question of Shelley: Unresolved Problems

When Joseph Arnould wrote to Alfred Domett in September, 1847, he mentioned *Pauline*, a poem written by their mutual friend Robert Browning and published anonymously in 1833. Arnould's comment on the poem is extremely perceptive: he called it "a strange, wild (in parts singularly magnificent) poet-biography: his own early life as it presented itself to his own soul viewed poetically: in fact, psychologically speaking, his 'Sartor Resartus': it was written and published three [two] years before 'Paracelsus,' when Shelley was his God."[1] It is therefore not surprising that W. C. DeVane quotes Arnould in the section of his *Browning Handbook* devoted to the poem, and that DeVane himself echoes Arnould's appraisal: "*Pauline* is much more than a song in honor of Shelley: it is in a wider sense Browning's autobiography to his twentieth year, at once his *Sartor Resartus* and his *Prelude*."[2]

Although both of these statements are acceptable generalities, there is one essential difference between *Pauline* and the two works which it so closely resembles, *Sartor Resartus* and *The Prelude*. Carlyle and Wordsworth had written studies in self-discovery only after they had attained some degree of emotional and mental maturity. In each case, the articulation of past personal difficulties is accompanied by a note of assurance that the problem, whether it be Teufelsdröckh's loss of Blumine's love in Book III, Chapter V, of *Sartor*, or Wordsworth's loss of imaginative power in Book XII of the *Prelude*, has been solved and can now be discussed with relative objectivity. But Browning's exercise in self-exposure, written when he was twenty years old,

[1] *Robert Browning and Alfred Domett*, ed. F. G. Kenyon (London: Smith, Elder, 1906), p. 141.

[2] *A Browning Handbook* (2d ed.; New York: Appleton-Century-Crofts, 1955), p. 44.

does not leave one with the impression that the author knows where he has been, understands where he is, and has definite plans as to where he is going.

This uncertainty was recognized by John Stuart Mill, who also discussed *Pauline*, in his well-known unpublished review written in 1833, in terms applicable to *Sartor Resartus*.[3] Mill notes, however, that the unknown author of the poem has not progressed much beyond the "Everlasting No" stage, in which problems are articulated but not resolved:

> With considerable poetic powers, the writer seems to me possessed with a more intense and morbid self-consciousness than I ever knew in any sane human being. I should think it a sincere confession, though of a most unlovable state, if the "Pauline" were not evidently a mere phantom. All about her is full of inconsistency . . . . A cento of most beautiful passages might be made from this poem, and the psychological history of himself is powerful and truthful—*truth-like* certainly, all but the last stage. *That*, he evidently has not yet got into. The self-seeking and self-worshipping state is well described—beyond that, I should think the writer had made, as yet, only the next step, viz. into despising his own state. I even question whether part even of that self-disdain is not *assumed*. He is evidently *dissatisfied*, and feels part of the badness of his state; he does not write as if it were purged out of him. If he once could muster a hearty hatred of his selfishness it would *go*; as it is, he feels only the *lack* of *good*, not the positive evil. He feels not remorse, but only disappointment; a mind in that state can only be regenerated by some new passion, and I know not what to wish for him but that he may meet with a *real* Pauline.
>
> Meanwhile he should not attempt to show how a person may be *recovered* from this morbid state,—for *he* is hardly convalescent, and "what should we speak of but that which we know?"[4]

The absence of mental and emotional discipline perceived by Mill is apparent in the very structure of the poem itself—a series of moods and mental states strung together with little coherence, interrupted by strikingly beautiful lyric flights, a long eulogy to Shelley, and rounded off with talk of love to the imaginary Pauline which ranges from passionate physical desire to spiritual idolatry. That the unnamed

[3] See Lewis F. Haines, "Mill and *Pauline*: The 'Review' that 'Retarded Browning's Fame,'" *Modern Language Notes*, LXIX (1944), 410–412.

[4] Quoted by W. H. Griffin and H. C. Minchin in *The Life of Robert Browning* (New York: Macmillan, 1910), pp. 59–60.

poet-hero, who serves as a thin disguise for Browning throughout the poem, recognizes his own obtuseness and lack of stability is evident in his repeated apologies to Pauline:

> I have no confidence,
> So I will sing on—fast as fancies come
> Rudely—the verse being as the mood it paints.
>
> (ll. 257–259)

> Thou know'st, dear friend, I could not think all calm,
> For wild dreams followed me, and bore me off,
> And all was indistinct. Ere one was caught
> Another glanced; so dazzled by my wealth,
> Knowing not which to leave nor which to choose,
> For all my thoughts so floated, nought was fixed.
>
> (ll. 877–882)[5]

If *Pauline* is to be correctly understood in the context of Browning's development, it must be seen for what it is; that is, it must be considered not only in light of the comments by Arnould and DeVane, but also from the point of view suggested by John Stuart Mill. *Pauline* is a review of Browning's life and development up to 1833; but, equally important, because the author has not yet "recovered" from the morbid state he describes, it reflects the causes, the unresolved problems, which have given rise to that state. The nature of these problems is indicated by the young poet's ambiguous attitude toward Shelley, the "Sun-treader," and the unconvincing tone of the religious resolution and the rejection of selfishness which occurs in the final stages of the poem.[6] In *Pauline*, Browning is unable to define clearly his attitude

---

[5] *Pauline by Robert Browning: The Text of 1833, Compared With That of 1867 and 1888*, ed. N. Hardy Wallis (London: University of London Press, 1931). All citations from *Pauline* are from this edition.

[6] DeVane recognizes the difficulty of Shelley's position in the poem, although I do not think that he places sufficient emphasis on how this affects the poem's conclusion, or why it is significant: "In *Pauline* he represents himself as having escaped from the subversive religious thought of Shelley; but surely not before 1855 was he free from the poetic thought of the Sun-treader, if indeed he ever entirely escaped. The glorious discovery is chronicled in *Pauline*, and it is significant that Browning there at once repudiates and yet follows adoringly his master. It is enough to say here that Shelley made Browning the poet he was; he gave him poetical and political ideas, method and technique, and pointed out that the proper subject of poetry is the soul of the poet himself" (*Handbook*, pp. 9–10). The

toward either Shelley or God, and this in turn reflects the confusion in his own mind concerning the nature of both poetry and religion and their relationship to one another.

At three separate points in the poem, Browning expresses his love for Shelley as it exists in 1833 when the poem is being written. Yet in the section of *Pauline* written in the past tense, in which Browning records his own poetic development, he explains that sometime before 1833 he rejected Shelley because of his atheism and the impracticality of his utopian ideals. To further complicate the question of his attitude toward Shelley, Browning states at the conclusion of the poem that he places his trust in God, but in the same line he mentions Shelley with equal reverence. This declaration of contrary allegiances invalidates what might otherwise have been a convincing religious conclusion to the poem.

*Pauline* solves none of the questions it raises, but by presenting conflicting attitudes toward Shelley, and thereby obscuring the religious resolution of the poem, *Pauline* does point to the terms within which Browning will work—indeed, within which he must work if he is ever to write meaningful poetry—in his next two major poems, *Paracelsus* and *Sordello*. In *Paracelsus*, Browning relegates his confused attitude toward Shelley, and therefore poetry, to a secondary position, and concentrates on defining and clarifying his moral ideas. And, having established these basic moral ideas, he then proceeds in *Sordello* to examine his aesthetic theory in considerable detail. By 1840, the unresolved problems concerning poetry and morality which plagued Browning in *Pauline* have been faced realistically and defined with relative clarity. But to understand why it was necessary for Browning to turn to the investigation of moral and aesthetic questions after *Pauline*, it is first necessary to see how muddled his conception of these subjects was in 1833. This confusion is illustrated in the contradictory allusions to Shelley in *Pauline*, and in the fact that the basic contradictions in his attitude toward Shelley weaken the force of the statement of religious dedication which closes the poem.

Browning's first allusion to Shelley in *Pauline* is full of the confused syntax which pervades the poem and which, one can conjecture,

"technique" which Browning drew upon from Shelley's *Alastor* for *Pauline* is discussed by Park Honan in *Browning's Characters: A Study In Poetic Technique* (New Haven: Yale University Press, 1961), pp. 11–17.

reflects the author's own mental state. As he looks back on his youth, Browning remembers those "rude songs" and "wild imaginings" which now seem "most distinct amid / The fever and the stir of after years!" (ll. 139–140), and expresses his gratitude to Shelley for the memory of that youthful exuberance. He then proceeds to castigate Shelley's unkind critics, attributing to that poet a power of aloofness from criticism which cannot be shared by those who are in his debt:

> I ne'er had ventured e'en to hope for this,
> Had not the glow I felt at HIS award,
> Assured me all was not extinct within.
> HIM whom all honor—whose renown springs up
> Like sunlight which will visit all the world;
> So that e'en they who sneered at him at first,
> Come out to it, as some dark spider crawls
> From his foul nets, which some lit torch invades,
> Yet spinning still new films for his retreat.—
> Thou didst smile, poet,—but, can *we* forgive?
>
> (ll. 141–150)

N. Hardy Wallis brings out the problematical aspects of this passage in his "Analytical Notes," by questioning the reference of the capitalized pronouns: "To whom does the 'His' refer? If to the Deity, what is the significance of line 150? If, however, it refers to Shelley, which would be consistent with the address to him which follows, why has the writer placed both pronouns in capitals?"[7] A tentative answer to this query might be that Browning, by capitalizing "HIS" and "HIM," is attempting to indicate how closely God and Shelley (or the concept of poetry represented by Shelley), seemed to be bound up to him as a youth. At any rate, the unmitigated praise of the apostrophe which follows immediately after these lines leaves little doubt of the young poet's attitude toward Shelley, at least in this part of the poem:

> Sun-treader—life and light be thine for ever;
> Thou art gone from us—years go by—and spring
> Gladdens, and the young earth is beautiful,
> Yet thy songs come not—other bards arise,
> But none like thee.
>
> (ll. 151–155)

---

[7] *Pauline*, p. 77.

The reason Browning gives for recalling his lost youth, and the sanative influence of Shelley which is so intimately connected with that period of joy, is made clear in the complaint to Pauline which typifies his present state of despair. That time of peace, when the poet sang to and for mankind, is gone. He has "chosen gifts / Distinct from theirs" (ll. 80–81), and his soul has

> floated from its sphere
> Of wild dominion into the dim orb
> Of self . . .
> It has conformed itself to that dim orb,
> Reflecting all its shades and shapes, and now
> Must stay where it alone can be adored.
>
> (ll. 90–95)

Although this egocentricity has divorced him from Shelley, Browning can nevertheless remember what his idol once was to him, and can still reverence that memory:

> The air seems bright with thy past presence yet,
> But thou art still for me, as thou hast been
> When I have stood with thee, as on a throne
> With all thy dim creations gathered round
> Like mountains,—and I felt of mould like them,
> And creatures of my own were mixed with them,
> Like things half-lived, catching and giving life.
>
> (ll. 161–167)

However, he cannot act upon his love of Shelley to save himself:

> And I, perchance, half feel a strange regret,
> That I am not what I have been to thee.
>
> (ll. 191–192)

Browning concludes the eulogy with a contrast between Shelley and himself which further depicts his own helpless state and at the same time adds to the rendition of Shelley's qualities. The poet figure of *Pauline* affirms that he now has nothing in common with his mentor. The beauteous "shapes" of Shelley's poetry elude him; foul forms seek him which could never approach Shelley. Knowing that he can no longer emulate Shelley, he resigns himself to the role of a "watcher" who, having debased himself through self-love, is "Altered, and worn, and weak, and full of tears" (l. 229).

The alleged purpose of *Pauline* is to enable the poet-hero who speaks throughout the poem to purge himself by the enunciation of his guilt. The form this confession finally takes, after approximately three hundred lines of wandering discourse, is a review of events which have preceded and caused the poet's crisis of soul. It is not until the second third of the poem, from lines 318 to 715, that an organizing chronological principle is employed, and in this section the most obvious references to Browning's own past are found.[8] The attitude toward Shelley in this section of *Pauline* completely contradicts the all-embracing devotion professed in the "Sun-treader" lines discussed above.

The eulogy in which the "Sun-treader" lines occur is written in the present tense, and after reading it one cannot help but believe that the author is wholly dedicated to Shelley at the time he is composing the poem ("other bards arise / But none like thee," "thou art still for me, as thou hast been"). However, in the biographical section of *Pauline*, Browning, writing in the past tense, relates that at some time prior to the composition of this poem he had become enamored of Shelley, subjected himself to that poet's ideas for a time, and then become completely disillusioned with him. This depiction of Browning's relationship with Shelley, outlined in the second movement of *Pauline*, is confirmed by biographical data.

Until 1826, when he was fourteen years old, Browning seems to have accepted the Non-Conformist faith of his mother and, although not always the model of deportment at services, did accompany her to York Street Chapel. At fourteen, however, he discovered Voltaire in his father's library and, at about the same time, received a copy of Shelley's *Miscellaneous Poems*, published by Benbow, from his cousin James Silverthorn.[9] The effect of Voltaire and Shelley on the young Browning was immediate and intense. We are told by Mrs. Sutherland Orr that "the earliest result of the new development was that he became a professing atheist, and, for two years, a practising vegetarian," and that he "gratuitously proclaimed himself everything that he was,

---

[8] See Griffin and Minchin, *The Life of Robert Browning*, pp. 41–60, and DeVane's *Handbook*, pp. 8–10, 42–44.

[9] For a full discussion of the poems of Shelley which Browning possessed in 1826, see Frederick A. Pottle's *Shelley and Browning: A Myth and Some Facts* (Chicago: Pembroke Press, 1923).

and some things he was not." [10] The vegetarian stage ceased in 1828 because Browning found his eyesight growing weak from a diet of bread and potatoes, but exactly when he decided that the diet of Shelley's atheism was as spiritually and poetically unrewarding as his vegetarianism was physically, is unknown. However, if we accept as fact Browning's own statement in the biographical portion of *Pauline* concerning the circumstances which led up to Shelley's influence, and the description of the nature of that influence itself, we can only conclude that the decision to reject Shelley was made before 1833.

In *Pauline*, Browning's review of the time leading up to the phase of Shelley's influence begins with the mention of those "wisest ancient books" (l. 319), specified as the *Iliad* (l. 325), Plato (l. 435), Aeschylus' *Agamemnon* (l. 567), and Sophocles' *Oedipus* (l. 573), which he found in his father's large collection. [11] His poetic impulses were aroused by this reading and, through a power of imaginative identification maturely demonstrated in the later historical monologues, he

> went with the tale—a god,
> Wandering after beauty—or a giant,
> Standing vast in the sunset—an old hunter,
> Talking with gods—or a high-crested chief,
> Sailing with troops of friends to Tenedos;—
> I tell you, nought has ever been so clear
> As the place, the time, the fashion of those lives.
>
> (ll. 321–327)

Following the description of a period of "long restraint" (ll. 344–356), which, according to DeVane's speculation, refers to the "unlovely aspect of his boyish nature" when he left school as an "aggressive, self-confident, and not a little self-centered" [12] youth, Browning alludes to his first attempt at poetic apprenticeship as one in which

> No fear was mine
> As I gazed on the works of mighty bards,
> In the first joy at finding my own thoughts
> Recorded, and my powers exemplified,
> And feeling their aspirings were my own.
>
> (ll. 384–388)

[10] *Life and Letters of Robert Browning* (Boston, 1891), I, 59, 64.
[11] DeVane, *Handbook*, p. 44.
[12] *Ibid.*, p. 6.

This was a period of imitation: "I rather sought / To rival what I wondered at" (ll. 390–391)—which probably refers to Byron and the *Incondita* volume containing Browning's two earliest extant poems, "The First Born of Egypt" and "The Dance of Death."[13]

But the desire for mere technical imitation was soon extinct. With the quickening of his poetic powers and the passing of boyhood, "restraints" were no longer acceptable to the youth who sought a philosophic system which would satisfy his adolescent yearning for freedom. That "vague sense of powers folded up," which had made him feel that "I should rule" (ll. 341–343), required liberation and realization. At this stage, susceptibility to the high-sounding melioristic doctrines of Shelley was naturally very great:

> I dreamed not of restraint, but gazed
> On all things: schemes and systems went and came,
> And I was proud (being vainest of the weak),
> In wandering o'er them, to seek out some one
> To be my own; as one should wander o'er
> The white way for a star.
>
> On one, whom praise of mine would not offend,
> Who was as calm as beauty.
>
> (ll. 398–405)[14]

What drew the young Browning to Shelley was his impression of the poet's selfless belief in and devotion to mankind, his efforts at winning them "back to peace," and, the reader is led to suspect, his

13 *New Poems by Robert Browning and Elizabeth Barrett Browning*, ed. F. G. Kenyon (London: Smith, Elder, 1914), pp. 3–12. Concerning the Byronic influence, Mrs. Orr reports that she was told the volume was a product of the period "when he was only twelve, in which the Byronic influence was predominant" (*Life and Letters*, I, 46).

14 The appellation "Sun-treader" is not used in this section of the poem, but three things suggest that the passage does refer to Shelley: first, the concepts attributed to this "one" (i.e., liberty and revolution—perhaps reflecting Browning's reading of *Prometheus Unbound*); second, the star image in line 403, which parallels the reference in line 171, "thou wert as a star to men" (see C. Willard Smith, *Browning's Star-Imagery* [Princeton: Princeton University Press, 1941], pp. 7–16); and third, the textual clarification added by Browning in the 1867 edition of the poem:

> as one should wander o'er
> The white way for a star. And my choice fell
> Not so much on a system as a man.

potentiality for fame and respect among fellow mortals (ll. 419–421). In 1826, at fourteen years of age, Browning dedicated himself to adoration of Shelley and to the fulfillment of Shelley's poetic mission:

> I was vowed to liberty,
> Men were to be as gods, and earth as heaven.
> And I—ah! what a life was mine to be,
> My whole soul rose to meet it.
>
> (ll. 424–427)

Unfortunately, such idealistic dreams came no truer for Browning than they did for Shelley. One who thinks he sees "A key to a new world" and thinks he hears "the muttering / Of angels" (ll. 414–415) in the work of another poet is, Browning implies, bound to be disillusioned. Browning's own awakening came when, after digesting the theoretical aspects of his poet-redeemer's creed, he proceeded to the world of real life to look upon men with "their cares, and hopes, and fears, and joys" and sought to discover "How best life's end might be attained" (ll. 443–445). In one of the most beautiful lyric passages of the poem, Browning explains what it is to discover the wide gulf which separates aspiration from achievement and theory from fact:

> And suddenly, without heart-wreck, I awoke
> As from a dream—I said, 'twas beautiful,
> Yet but a dream; and so adieu to it.
> As some world-wanderer sees in a far meadow
> Strange towers, and walled gardens, thick with trees,
> Where singing goes on, and delicious mirth,
> And laughing fairy creatures peeping over,
> And on the morrow, when he comes to live
> For ever by those springs, and trees, fruit-flushed
> And fairy bowers—all his search is vain.
>
> (ll. 447–456)

The effect of this sudden shattering of his dream to cure all the ills of mankind moves the poet from a state of extreme optimism to one of extreme pessimism. Hopes of perfecting mankind, the belief in freedom, in virtue, and in human love, are supplanted by wit, mockery, and jocular cynicism. God becomes a reflection of himself; his mind becomes a temple where "troops of shadows" (l. 474) kneel and

proclaim "thou art our king!" (l. 487). In the remainder of this section
of the poem, the hero describes to Pauline the various means he has
considered employing to efface the despair this disillusionment has
occasioned. Retreat into seclusion, the search for fame, a reversion to
the carefree irresponsibility of childhood, and the suppression of
passion have each been contemplated and in turn rejected. Finally,
realizing his weakness, instability, and selfishness, he considers the
possibility of taking refuge in the beauty of mythology. But this
solution is also judged inadequate.

In the initial phase of the last movement of the poem, beginning at
line 716, the poet experiences a sudden elevation of spirit, and begins
to identify himself with nature. After a long lyric passage which
celebrates nature's revivifying power, the hero of *Pauline* comes to
understand that for true regeneration he must subordinate his desires
to the will of God. He fights free from doubt, disillusionment, and
vacillation, to a religious affirmation which seems to fulfill his recognition, stated in the early lines of the poem, that in order to escape
extreme self-involvement and dissipation of mind he must accept God
as his "lode-star" and fulfill "A need, a trust, a yearning after God"
(ll. 292–295), which he had previously neglected. That desire is
apparently achieved when, in the final stages of the confession, he
asserts his dependence on God and Christ:

> And what is that I hunger for but God?
> My God, my God! let me for once look on thee
> As tho' nought else existed: we alone.
> And as creation crumbles, my soul's spark
> Expands till I can say, "Even from myself
> "I need thee, and I feel thee, and I love thee;
> "I do not plead my rapture in thy works
> "For love of thee—or that I feel as one
> "Who cannot die—but there is that in me
> "Which turns to thee, which loves, or which should love."
>
> . . . . . . . . . . . . .
>
> Is it not in my nature to adore,
> And e'en for all my reason do I not
> Feel him, and thank him, and pray to him?—*Now*.
> Can I forego the trust that he loves me?
>
> (ll. 821–836)

The religious statement Browning makes in these lines would seem entirely convincing, if it were possible to forget that in succeeding lines of *Pauline* he reverts again to the praise of Shelley as "Sun-treader" and addresses Shelley and God in the same breath and with equal reverence:

> Sun-treader, I believe in God, and truth,
> And love; and as one just escaped from death
> Would bind himself in bands of friends to feel
> He lives indeed—so, I would lean on thee;
> Thou must be ever with me—most in gloom
> When such shall come—but chiefly when I die,
> For I seem dying, as one going in the dark
> To fight a giant.
>
> (ll. 1020–1027)

And even the concluding statement on the nature of the poet seems to be little more than an echo of Shelleyan devotion:

> and I shall live
> With poets—calmer—purer still each time,
> And beauteous shapes will come to me again,
> And unknown secrets will be trusted me,
> Which were not mine when wavering—but now
> I shall be priest and lover, as of old.
>
> (ll. 1014–1019)[15]

Mrs. Betty Miller, in her *Robert Browning: A Portrait*, sets out to show that Browning was a psychological weakling whose main problem in life was reconciling himself to the domination of his mother. Her brief comment on *Pauline*, designed to elucidate this thesis, involves what she terms a conflict between "head" and "heart," that is, Browning's struggle in making a choice between the godlessness of Shelley and the godliness of his mother.[16] Although it is clear that

[15] In the 1888 edition, as if to emphasize the point, Browning changed the "lover" of line 1019 to "prophet."

[16] *Robert Browning: A Portrait* (New York: Charles Scribner's Sons, 1953), pp. 9–11. Why Mrs. Miller identifies Shelley with the "head," or reason, is unclear. In *Paracelsus* he seems to be identified with Aprile, or love. E. D. H. Johnson, in *The Alien Vision of Victorian Poetry* (Princeton: Princeton University Press, 1952), sees a conflict between "reason and instinct" in *Pauline*. And, although the conflict he discusses differs from that of Mrs. Miller, Johnson also contends that the poem achieves a clear resolution: "As a romantic assertion of the reality of the human

the resolution of the poem, and of the speaker's problems, does depend primarily on his assertion of a dependence on God, it is not equally clear that love of God and love of Shelley are irreconcilable opposites. Certainly the tendency of the thought in *Pauline* is toward religious faith and away from Shelley, but whether Browning clearly defined the nature of this conflict in the poem, or in his own mind by 1833, is quite a different matter. It is obvious to the critic who has read Browning's later work that the Shelleyan idealism was tempered by the poet's own peculiar brand of religious faith and by his poetic aims, but to state that "the ideals of Shelley and those of Sarah Anna Browning could not continue to exist under the same roof: the moment had come in which he must either deny his 'wild dreams of beauty and of good,' or irreparably wound and alienate his mother," [17] is attributing to *Pauline* a clarity it does not have, and to Browning a maturity that he had not attained in 1833. Indeed, it was this very lack of clarity in *Pauline* which led Browning to speculate more fully on these problems in later poems.

At best, one can say, in agreement with John Stuart Mill, that the last stage of the poem is a stage which Browning "evidently has not yet got into." [18] He distrusts Shelley's atheism and utopianism, but he continues to praise Shelley as his idol. He resolves to place his trust in

---

emotions, in opposition to the delusory processes of ratiocination, *Pauline* establishes a point of view which dominates all Browning's subsequent thinking" (p. 72). Norton B. Crowell, in *The Triple Soul: Browning's Theory of Knowledge* (Albuquerque: University of New Mexico Press, 1963), employs terminology similar to Miller's, but reaches a conclusion which is different from either Miller's or Johnson's: "The intellect is an imperfect instrument, as is everything in the mortal state, but it is indispensable. Only if it tyrannizes over the heart or aspires to knowledge of the infinite is it a snake in the beautiful garden" (p. 126).

[17] Miller, *A Portrait*, p. 11.

[18] Masao Miyoshi, in "Mill and 'Pauline': The Myth and Some Facts," *Victorian Studies*, IX (December 1965), 154–163, proposes that Mill's reading of the last section of *Pauline* is "erroneous" because in it the narrator states that he rejects the extreme egotism of the poem's earlier sections. But Mill's point is that there is a disharmony in the poem between the narrator's statement that a cure has been effected, and his inability to present a convincing illustration, by means of a consistently mature attitude, that the statement is true. And Browning's almost simultaneous declaration of allegiance to Shelley and God does suggest a lack of harmony, despite the confident tone in which that allegiance is expressed, and despite Miyoshi's belief that *Pauline*, in its "anti-Romantic resolution," represents "the Victorian descent into the here and now" (p. 163).

God, but the simple assertion of faith at the end of the poem is insufficient proof that he understands how faith in God is to affect his life as a poet and his artistic principles.

It is around these two poles of interest—Shelley and God—that *Pauline* revolves. And it must be stressed that the poem continues to revolve to the very last line; it does not stop, as Mrs. Miller would have us believe, at either one of these poles. At no point in the poem is it clear that Browning declares a final allegiance to either Shelley or God, or that he consciously faces the necessity of choosing between dedication to poetry or to religion. What is clear, however, is that Shelley and God are representative of whole areas of thought which Browning had not yet carefully explored when he wrote *Pauline*. The contradictory statements concerning Shelley, and the inadequacy of the religious dedication, indicate that in 1833 Browning's thoughts concerning aesthetic and moral theory were confused and even somewhat naive. And it is this intellectual confusion, even more than the structural disorder of the poem, which makes *Pauline* such an incomprehensible puzzle. The poet speaks to his lover Pauline in a tone which conveys, at points, the impression of adult authority and assurance, but what he says reveals that he is still caught in the throes of intellectual adolescence.

*Pauline* is, then, not basically a poem which defines ideas, but one in which a number of unresolved problems are set forth and complicated by autobiographical material. It is therefore hardly surprising that when Browning republished the poem in 1867, he added a note which read, in part, "The first piece in the series [*Pauline*], I acknowledge and retain with extreme repugnance.... The thing was my earliest attempt at 'poetry always dramatic in principle, and so many utterances of so many imaginary persons, not mine,'... good draughtsmanship, however, and right handling were far beyond the artist at that time."[19] The time would soon come, however, in *Paracelsus* and *Sordello*, when questions asked but not satisfactorily answered in *Pauline* would be investigated more fully, and when areas of thought opened up in *Pauline* would be more thoroughly examined.

[19] *Pauline*, p. xi.

## CHAPTER TWO

# *Paracelsus*: the Process of Moral Definition

*Paracelsus* was published in August, 1835, and was, according to Browning, written in less than six months.[1] Although *Pauline* had received a few favorable reviews, one of which Browning had petitioned for,[2] the general tenor of Mill's comments, in addition to the denigrating remarks published in *Fraser's Magazine*, *The Literary Gazette*, and *Tait's Edinburgh Magazine*, were of sufficient force and abusiveness to make Browning somewhat hesitant to publish another such confusing, self-revealing work.[3] *Paracelsus* represents

[1] W. C. DeVane, *A Browning Handbook* (2d ed.; New York: Appleton-Century-Crofts, 1955), pp. 49–50.

[2] For Browning's correspondence with W. J. Fox, editor of the *Monthly Repository*, see Mrs. Sutherland Orr, *Life and Letters of Robert Browning* (Boston, 1891), I, 77–81. Fox answered Browning's polite request for notice with an over-enthusiastic review which included the following remarkable prediction: "We felt certain of Tennyson, before we saw the book, by a few verses which had straggled into a newspaper; we are not less certain of the author of Pauline" (*Monthly Repository*, N.S. VII [April 1833], 262). Favorable reviews (i.e., qualified praise of *Pauline*, accompanied by recognition of the immature poet's potential genius) also appeared in the *Atlas* (April 14, 1833), p. 228, and the *Athenaeum* (April 6, 1833), p. 216.

[3] If Browning read these reviews, it is not surprising that he tried to remove the personal element from his poetry by adapting the life of a real historical figure to his own purposes in *Paracelsus*, and also in *Sordello*. "We have already had a *Monomaniac*; and we designate you 'The Mad Poet of the Batch'; as being mad not in one direction only, but in all. A little lunacy, like a little knowledge, would be a dangerous thing" ("The Poets of the Day: Batch the Third," *Fraser's Magazine*, XLVIII [December 1833], 669–670). "Somewhat mystical, somewhat poetical, somewhat sensual, and not a little unintelligible,—this is a dreamy volume, without an object, and unfit for publication" (*The Literary Gazette* [March 23, 1833], p. 183). "A piece of pure bewilderment..." (*Tait's Edinburgh Magazine*, III [August 1833], 668). Although it is difficult to document Browning's reaction to the critical reception of his first published work, it is probable that his shift to a more objective mode in *Paracelsus* was influenced by the accumulation of negative criticism which greeted *Pauline*, rather than solely by Mill's comments. See Masao Miyoshi's "Mill and 'Pauline': The Myth and Some Facts," *Victorian Studies*, IX (December 1965), 154–163.

Browning's attempt to escape the technical and ideological immaturity of *Pauline*.

This shift of attitude that occurred between 1833 and 1835 can be detected in the difference in tone between the Latin preface to *Pauline*, which conveys a condescendingly playful challenge to the reader—"I have no doubt that the title of our book may by its unusual character entice very many to read it, and that among them some of biased opinions, with weak minds—many even hostile and churlish—will attack our genius, who in the rashness of their ignorance will cry out, almost before they have read the title, that we are teaching forbidden things, are scattering the seeds of heresies . . ." [4]—and the humble, apologetic explanation of purpose and method which precedes *Paracelsus*:

> I am anxious that the reader should not, at the very outset—mistaking my performance for one of a class with which it has nothing in common—judge it by principles on which it was never moulded, and subject it to a standard to which it was never meant to conform. I therefore anticipate his discovery, that it is an attempt . . . to reverse the method usually adopted by writers whose aim it is to set forth any phenomenon of the mind or the passions, by the operation of persons and events; and . . . instead of having recourse to an external machinery of incidents to create and evolve the crisis I desire to produce, I have ventured to display somewhat minutely the mood itself in its rise and progress, and have suffered the agency by which it is influenced and determined, to be generally discernible in its effects alone, and subordinate throughout . . . . I trust for his [the reader's] indulgence towards a poem which had not been imagined six months ago . . . . [5]

But despite Browning's plea for "indulgence," the critical reader can only conclude that *Paracelsus* is no greater a technical success than *Pauline*. Park Honan's summary statement accurately describes the numerous ways in which *Paracelsus* "fails as a work of art":

> The truth is that *Paracelsus*, like *Pauline*, is more interesting and significant for the ways in which it abjectly fails as a work of art than for the charming ways in which it succeeds. It cannot be taken seriously as any

[4] DeVane, *Handbook*, pp. 41–42.

[5] *Paracelsus*, preface, pp. vii–ix. Citations from *Paracelsus* are from the unnumbered text *Paracelsus* (London, 1835). Line numbers have been added to facilitate comparison with the numbered text of the standard edition, *The Works of Robert Browning* (*Centenary Edition*), ed. F. G. Kenyon, 10 vols. (London: Smith, Elder, 1912).

kind of dramatic poem; it is almost incomprehensible as a portrait of the historical Paracelsus; it is too vague, too abstract, too greatly lacking in concrete references and details of any sort to "set forth [a] phenomenon of the mind or the passions"; it suffers moreover from the almost total absence not only of action in the ordinary sense, but of dramatic tension .... Lastly, it is disjointed ....[6]

There is, however, one important point of contrast between *Pauline* and *Paracelsus*: the ideas in *Pauline* are unclear, irresolute, and incomplete; in *Paracelsus*, on the other hand, the ideas are relatively clear, certain, and complete. And this difference is particularly significant, for in *Paracelsus* Browning is dealing with basically the same problems which had concerned him in *Pauline*. Browning's own development is described in *Pauline* as a series of stages. He desires greatness, pursues a utopian dream, fails, becomes a cynic, and finally announces that he is saved. But the conclusion of the poem, its religious resolution, is problematical and contradictory because, as Mill notes, Browning is too involved in the problems of his hero. Because he projects himself into the "I" of the poem, because he *is* the hero, Browning is unable to see himself, or his dilemma, objectively.

Although *Paracelsus* is not a technical success by any conceivable standard of critical judgment, Browning does achieve, through his experiment with form, a detachment which represents an advance on his part from the total personal involvement of *Pauline*. Whereas *Pauline* is lyric, *Paracelsus* is semidramatic. The first-person narrator of *Pauline* gives way to Paracelsus, Aprile, Festus, and Michal, who are manipulated by Browning to serve his own specific purposes. And because he is one step removed from his own problems in *Paracelsus*, Browning can work out, with a greater degree of objectivity, the moral dilemma left unsolved in *Pauline*: What is man's relationship to God and to his fellow man; how can unlimited aspiration be reconciled to limited ability; how can man reach God without succumbing to the fruitless idealism of Shelley; and how does one serve the human race without being dragged down into the quagmire of reality?

Browning's critics have generally accepted *Paracelsus* as an important document in the development of the poet's thought. W. O. Raymond, in "Browning's Conception of Love as Represented in

[6] *Browning's Characters: A Study in Poetic Technique* (New Haven: Yale University Press, 1961), p. 28.

'Paracelsus,'" writes that "though the poem was composed in his twenty-third year, Browning may be said to have established definitely in it the basis of his reflective thought on the fundamental problems of humanity.... While further elaborated in his later works and given a different setting, practically all of the leading and controlling ideas of his poetry are present in *Paracelsus*."[7]

An elucidation of Browning's "reflective thought on the fundamental problems of humanity" as it is worked out and defined in *Paracelsus* is important, for the "fundamental problems of humanity" are the fundamental problems of Browning himself. As DeVane notes, the poem is "something of a young man's prospectus of life—he sends Paracelsus and Aprile like spies before him into the strange land."[8] And, to continue the simile, the only way to understand the nature and significance of the destination the spies reach is to follow them in their course through the successive stages of the journey. The journey is, in fact, as important as the destination, for it becomes increasingly clear, after a careful reading of *Pauline*, *Paracelsus*, and *Sordello*, that Browning himself made the same mental journey not once, but three times before 1840.

CANTO ONE: "PARACELSUS ASPIRES"

The first scene of *Paracelsus* takes place in the year 1507 in a garden at Würzburg. Paracelsus is preparing to embark on his quest, the proposed end of which is

> to comprehend the works of God,
> And God himself, and all God's intercourse
> With our own mind.

(I.553–555)

In the opening speech of the poem, as Paracelsus takes leave of Festus and Festus' betrothed, Michal, the theme of love is introduced in terms of the relationship which exists between Paracelsus and his friends. Paracelsus compares himself to autumn:

---

[7] In *The Infinite Moment and Other Essays in Robert Browning* (2d ed.; Toronto: University of Toronto Press, 1965), p. 156. See also Stopford A. Brooke's *The Poetry of Robert Browning* (London: Isbister, 1902), pp. 14–15, and Hugh Walker's *The Greater Victorian Poets* (London, 1895), p. 37.

[8] *Handbook*, p. 50.

Autumn would fain be sunny—*I* would look
Liker my nature's truth; and both are frail,
And both beloved for all their frailty!

(I.20–22)

Like autumn, Paracelsus wishes to be loved and remembered by his
friends. But despite his apparent recognition, at this early stage, of the
value of love, Paracelsus has no true conception of what love means or
what it involves. This is suggested by the method he desires to use to
prove his great love for his friends. Rather than regarding love as a
power of sympathy and reciprocal understanding, Paracelsus considers
it only as something which can serve as a mirror of his own great
powers. He could best prove his love by listening to Festus' misgivings
about his quest for knowledge. However, Paracelsus is far above such
simplicity; he would have Festus "Devise some test of love—some
arduous feat / To be perform'd" (I.117–118) in order to prove his
affection.

In answer to Festus' entreaty to renounce the task he has set for
himself, Paracelsus replies that he cannot abandon the sole end for
which he lives. He cannot "Reject God's great commission" (I.148).
Here we are given the first indication of Paracelsus' greatest fault, his
pride. He implies that it is not as a result of his own desires that he
seeks "to KNOW" (I.301), but because he has been chosen for the
task directly by God:

I profess no other share
In the selection of my lot, than in
My ready answer to the will of God,
Who summons me to be his organ.

(I.312–315)

Festus, the realist, recognizes the danger of Paracelsus' blatant self-love,
and charges that it is presumptuous for his friend to claim so direct a
relationship to God. He is further convinced of Paracelsus' pride in
achievement and desire for glory when he remembers the "hidden
scorn" and "That ready acquiescence in contempt" (I.281, 283)
which Paracelsus displayed when his knowledge surpassed that of his
fellow students at Einsiedeln.

With repeated warnings, Festus lays bare all the weaknesses of
Paracelsus' plan to attain infinite knowledge. First, Festus foresees

that as a result of his pride, Paracelsus will not accept the conventional means of ascertaining truth:

> There is a curse upon the earth; let man
> Presume not to serve God apart from such
> Appointed channel as he wills shall gather
> Imperfect tributes.
>
> (I.327–330)

Paracelsus' rejection of appointed channels will cause him to be completely divorced not only from past knowledge, but also from his fellow human beings:

> you have link'd to this, your enterprize,
> An arbitrary and most perplexing scheme
> Of seeking it in strange and untried paths;
> Rejecting past example, practice, precept—
> That so you may stand aidless and alone.
>
> (I.431–435)

Far from being discouraged by such a prospect, Paracelsus relates that when he first experienced the sublimity of divine vision, he "view'd the throng'd, / The ever-moving, concourse of mankind" (I.468–469) and realized that he could never join it. He must

> elevate [himself] far, far above
> The gorgeous spectacle; . . . longing
> To trample on yet save mankind at once.
>
> (I.479–481)

Clearly, Paracelsus aspires to become a type of exalted savior of mankind. He wishes to separate himself from the commonweal and the realm of mutual love in order to seek the splendor of ultimate knowledge in isolation. The intensity of Paracelsus' arrogance is shown when he announces what his reaction will be after he has achieved this knowledge and has deigned to share it with mankind:

> Once the feat achieved,
> I would withdraw from their officious praise,
> Would gently put aside their profuse thanks,
> Like some knight traversing a wilderness,
> Who, on his way, may chance to free a tribe
> Of desert-people from their dragon-foe.
>
> (I.491–496)

When Michal, with naive feminine admiration, exclaims that Paracelsus is "God's commissary! he shall / Be great and grand—and all for us!" (I.630–631), Paracelsus again reveals the depths of his pride by assuring his friends that even if he does succeed in helping mankind, he will remain constant to his desire for isolated grandeur: "If I can serve mankind / 'Tis well—but there our intercourse must end" (I.633–634). At this point, Festus again warns the philosopher of the imminent danger of a scheme based on such egotistical motives:

> Look well to this; *here* is a plague-spot, veil it,
> Disguise it how you will:
>
> . . . . . . . . . . .
>
> 'Tis but a spot as yet; but it will break
> Into a hideous blotch if overlook'd.
> How can that course be safe which from the first
> Produces carelessness to human love?
>
> (I.636–642)

Festus here anticipates the recognition of Paracelsus in Canto Two that love as well as knowledge is necessary for one who would seek to discover the secret of the universe. However, Festus stresses the necessity of *human* love, just as he has previously suggested that man should be content with "imperfect tributes" in his quest for knowledge.

Whereas Paracelsus is concerned solely with infinite knowledge, just as he will be concerned with infinite love in Canto Two, Festus understands the essential difference between what is accessible to man and what lies beyond his proper sphere of activity. The point of all Festus' warnings in Canto One is that Paracelsus aims at a goal which is unattainable to man. In the height of his idealism, Paracelsus accepts the value of the soul while rejecting the necessity of the flesh. This becomes particularly apparent when he enlarges upon his conception of knowledge:

> Truth is within ourselves; it takes no rise
> From outward things, whate'er you may believe:
> There is an inmost centre in us all,
> Where truth abides in fulness; and around,
> Wall within wall, the gross flesh hems it in,
> Perfect and true perception—which is truth;

A baffling and perverting carnal mesh
Which blinds it, and makes error: and, "*to know*"
Rather consists in opening out a way
Whence the imprison'd splendour may dart forth,
Than in effecting entry for the light
Supposed to be without.

(I.755–766)

I will learn
How to set free the soul alike in all,
By searching out the laws by which the flesh
Accloys the spirit.

(I.810–813)

Make no more giants, God!
But elevate the race at once!

.  .  .  .  .  .  .  .  .  .  .

See if we cannot beat thy angels yet!

(I.815–820)

These lines are illustrative of Paracelsus' attitude toward knowledge in Canto One. The purpose of knowledge is to liberate the truth which resides in man's "inmost centre." Paracelsus does not see truth as something external to man, but as a power of perception which resides in him; hence he sees no necessity of depending on anyone but himself in his quest for knowledge. Paracelsus, in seeking to "comprehend the works of God / And God himself" by liberating the vision of truth within his own being, implies that he is not only the possessor of knowledge, but its creator. Thus, in spite of the fact that he frequently mentions the word "God," one cannot help but suspect that in liberating this knowledge Paracelsus hopes to establish his own godhead. Furthermore, in his desire to attain the infinite, to "beat thy angels," he sees the flesh as nothing but a burden to the spirit. The flesh does not help soul; it is a "carnal mesh" which is the cause of all error. As Paracelsus later understands, the primary cause of his failure lies in the rejection of his own humanity. Even the simple Michal sees this: "Man should be humble; you are very proud!" (I.728). But despite their misgivings, Festus and Michal finally agree with Paracelsus that he is capable of accomplishing the task he has set himself, and he leaves Würzburg with complete confidence.

## CANTO TWO: "PARACELSUS ATTAINS"

Canto Two, which opens fourteen years after Paracelsus leaves Festus and Michal, can be divided into two parts. In the first section, Paracelsus, in a monologue, laments his lack of success in his quest for knowledge and dimly recalls his renunciation of love in Canto One. As shown below, a detailed explication of this passage reveals that Paracelsus actually does come very close to discovering that "the secret of the world" (I.295) lies in the acceptance of imperfect knowledge and imperfect love as the instruments man must use in attaining final communion with the Absolute. However, with the entrance of Aprile in the second section of the canto, Paracelsus loses these threads of thought and reverts to his quest for ultimates. Aprile states repeatedly that he would "love infinitely" (II.363), but he also adds that if he could have another chance to reach this goal he would not reject the "weeds," or the corresponding "imperfect tributes" of Festus, as he has done previously. Paracelsus, hypnotized by the words "love infinitely," misses Aprile's meaning, just as he has missed the significance of Festus' warnings in Canto One. The scene closes with Paracelsus' statement, "let *me* love! ... / I HAVE ATTAIN'D, AND NOW I MAY DEPART" (II.622–623). He goes forth again in error, this time strengthened by the hope that the combination of perfect knowledge with perfect love will ensure his success.

Paracelsus' monologue and his encounter with Aprile take place in the house of a Greek conjurer in Constantinople. The philosopher has come to a pause in his quest. He accepts the unhappy truth that the past fourteen years have contributed little to his search, and he realizes that his failure is partially due to his rejection of the incidental truths he has discovered while in the process of seeking perfect knowledge. The significance of what he has gained thus far is indicated by its place in the conjurer's book, "'twixt an ideot's [*sic*] gibber / And a mad lover's ditty" (II.32–33).

Paracelsus is so weary from his past toils, and so dejected from his present sense of failure, that he is willing to reject completely his initial aims. Originally he wanted to acquire divine knowledge; now he desires simply "to know my place, / My portion, my reward, even my failure" (II.68–69). And in this state of fatigued desperation, Paracelsus begins to think about the past. He attempts, in his bitterness, to shrug off the responsibility for his failure by blaming God: "At worst I have perform'd *my* share of the task. / The rest is God's concern" (II.89–90). Nevertheless, as he remembers his days at Würzburg with Festus and Michal, he does begin to acquire some insight into the cause of his failure. This approach to recognition on his part serves to strengthen the importance of Aprile's admonition shortly after and to emphasize the tragedy of Paracelsus' complete regression into blindness when the word "infinite" draws him back to his old goals.

Paracelsus thinks of the "parch'd sand-tract" (II.117) that his life has become, and he sadly recollects the grief that the rejection of love has caused him:

>                                        'tis very plain
> Some soft spots had their birth in me at first—
> If not love, say, like love: there was a time
> When yet this wolfish hunger after knowledge
> Set not remorselessly its claims aside;
> This heart was human once, or why recall
> Einsiedeln, even now, and Würzburg.
>                                        (II.120–126)

After reflecting on love—and it should be noted that he is here concerned with human love—Paracelsus proceeds to discuss the change which has taken place in his idea of knowledge:

>                          life, death, light, and shadow,
> The shows of the world, were bare receptacles
> Or indices of truth to be wrung thence,
> Not ministers of sorrow or delight—
> A wondrous natural robe in which I went:
> For some one truth would dimly beacon me
> From mountains rough with pines, and flit and wink
> O'er dazzling wastes of frozen snow, and tremble
> Into assured light in some branching mine,
> Where ripens, swathed in fire, the liquid gold—
> Yet all was then o'erlook'd, though noted now.
> So much is good, then, in this working sea
> Which parts me from that happy strip of land.
> But o'er that happy strip a sun shone too!
> And fainter gleams it as the waves grow rough,
> And still more faint as the sea widens. Last,

> I sicken on a dead gulf, streak'd with light
> From its own putrifying depths alone!
>
> (II.155–172)

The syntax of this passage makes an exact analysis somewhat difficult, but, recalling the attitude of Paracelsus toward knowledge in Canto One, the following interpretation seems most probable. At the beginning of his quest, life, death, light, shadow, and the wonders and beauties of nature were not important in themselves, but merely the external manifestation of some hidden inner truth. These "shows" were only "indices" which pointed to something more rewarding and, as such, could be ignored. Now, however, he is beginning to understand that worldly phenomena should be noted and utilized in one's attempt to fasten on the "liquid gold" which symbolizes the goal of his quest. He believes that this, at least, is some progress in his search for knowledge.

The lines containing the metaphor of the sea are more complex. To understand the meaning of the sea image in this passage, it is necessary to consider the significance of similar images which appear in Canto One. When Paracelsus questioned the purpose of Festus' warnings, Festus answered with a sea image. His advice was, he stated,

> A solitary briar the bank puts forth
> To save our swan's nest floating out to sea.
>
> (I.143–144)

In these lines, Paracelsus is spoken of as a swan's nest and his future realm of activity as a sea. The briar represents the warnings of Festus, who is referred to as the bank. A sea image is also used in the closing lines of Canto One. Paracelsus picks up Festus' allusion to his quest as a sea and, rejecting the swan image, romantically depicts himself as a beggar diving for a pearl:

> Are there not Festus . . .
> Two points in the adventure of the diver:
> One—when a beggar he prepares to plunge?
> One—when a prince he rises with his pearl?
>
> (I.868–871)

The use of these symbols in Canto One helps to clarify their meaning in Canto Two. Paracelsus speaks of the "working sea" (his quest), which parts him from "that happy strip of land." The strip of land in this case could refer to either of two things: what he has left behind (Würzburg, Festus, and Michal), or his final goal (infinite knowledge). However, since Festus referred to himself as the bank in Canto One, and since Paracelsus has been thinking about the past, Festus, and Michal, it seems most logical that the strip of land symbolizes the starting point of his journey, Würzburg. If this is true, it is perhaps also possible that the sun Paracelsus speaks of refers to the love of Festus and Michal or, for that matter, human love in general. This sun of love which Paracelsus rejected in Canto One grows fainter as his quest becomes more difficult. Now the only light he has rises from the "putrifying depths" of his own despair.

Paracelsus, then, in spite of the hopelessness of his present position, has learned something about the true nature of love and knowledge. Human love and the external phenomena which point to truth are becoming important for him. However, he has not progressed far enough to understand that these new insights must be applied to his own predicament. Instead, he unwillingly faces the possibility that he was never justified in his search for knowledge: "Ha, have I, after all, / Mistaken the wild nursling of my breast?" (II.218–219).[9] But the fear that this could be possible is too great for him. Rather than completely reject the validity of his past aims, he affirms his faith in God and the mind and accepts the fate God's will dictates:

> God! Thou art Mind! Unto the Master-Mind
> Mind should be precious. Spare my mind alone!
> All else I will endure.
>
> (II.225–227)

At this point of ready acceptance, Aprile enters. Like Paracelsus, who is stranded on a "dead gulf," Aprile is "Wreck'd on a savage isle" (II.464). Both figures have sought an impossible goal: Paracelsus "to KNOW," and Aprile to "love infinitely, and be loved" (II.370). Paracelsus, while seeking infinite knowledge, has rejected partial truths; Aprile, while seeking infinite love, has rejected the common joys of life. W. O. Raymond describes the idealistic philosophy of Aprile in Canto Two as follows:

[9] The reference of "nursling" is clarified in the 1849 revised edition by the following line, which Browning inserted after line 219: "Knowledge it seemed, and Power, and Recompense!"

The fine opening passages of the second canto of *Paracelsus*, where Aprile reveals his "mighty aim" and "full desire," portray love in the loftiest vein of romantic idealism. The love of the poet Aprile might be defined in the very words of Plato as "the desire of generation and production in the beautiful." Aprile would woo the loveliness of life through the medium of the creative genius of the artist. He yearns to reveal and transfigure the beauty of the natural world by reclothing it in the glorious forms of art. Thus his works would remain in the sight of all men, as pledges of the love which existed between himself and the beautiful. But, desiring to grasp the whole sum and absolute essence of beauty, he cannot rest content with any finite manifestation of it.[10]

Raymond makes the simple but perceptive suggestion that Aprile is closely modeled upon Browning's conception of Shelley. And although he does not deal extensively with *Pauline*, Raymond's analysis of Shelley's influence suggests a direct relationship between the creation of Aprile in *Paracelsus* and Browning's problem in the ambiguous handling of Shelley in the earlier work. Raymond writes:

The very creation of Aprile is undoubtedly to be traced to the influence of the personality and writings of Shelley upon Browning . . . . it seems unmistakable that he had Shelley vividly in mind in his portraiture of the spiritually impassioned seeker after absolute beauty . . . . The limitless aim, the eager craving after emotional experience, the exquisite sensitiveness, the single-hearted impulsiveness of Shelley, are reflected in Aprile. Shelley, like Aprile, eagle-winged in aspiration, had been dazzled by a vision of the infinite, and his lofty conception of love remaining merely nebulous, too often tended to dissipate itself in dreams and abstractions.[11]

As noted in Chapter One, the oversimplification sometimes applied to the Shelley-Browning relationship in *Pauline* is that Browning rejected the atheism of Shelley to return to the religion of his mother. But, as I have also attempted to show, there are a number of elements in *Pauline* which would seem to indicate that Browning had not defined the problem this clearly by 1833. If Raymond is correct about Aprile, it seems quite possible that in Canto Two Browning is consciously formulating his position with respect to Shelley more exactly than he could two years earlier. Shelley is dangerous not because of his atheism, but because his idealism is not grounded in

---

[10] *The Infinite Moment*, pp. 165–166.
[11] *Ibid.*, pp. 164–165.

reality. Such aspiration is self-destructive because, while its end may be valid, its means are negligent of reality in their complete denial of the human situation. The whole of *Paracelsus* is, in one sense, devoted to exploring the moral implications of Shelley's poetic influence, and his philosophic position as Browning saw it.

But since the character of Paracelsus was Browning's major concern in 1835, we find that Aprile is converted from Shelleyism in order to offer the philosopher Browning's solution to the problem of his quest. Aprile, on the point of death, admits that if he could have another chance to pursue love he would no longer reject the "frailest joy" (II.353) of life. He would glory in the imperfect, which is the proper sphere of imperfect man:

> I would adventure nobly for their [men's] sakes:
> .   .   .   .   .   .   .   .   .   .   .   .   .
> "In haste—not pausing to reject the weeds,
> "But happy plucking them at any price.
> "To me, who have seen them bloom in their own soil,
> "They are scarce lovely: plait and wear them you!
> .   .   .   .   .   .   .   .   .   .   .   .
>                     for common life, its wants
> And ways, would I set forth in beauteous hues.
>                                   (II.487–510)

Paracelsus, having prepared himself to accept Aprile's message in the first section of this canto, should now unhesitatingly grasp the solution which Aprile offers him; but the words "infinite love" have served to distract him from the true import of Aprile's speech, and his plea to the dying poet indicates that he has misinterpreted Aprile's warning:

> Die not, Aprile: we must never part.
> Are we not halves of one dissever'd world,
> Whom this strange chance unites once more?
>                     Part? never!
> Till thou, the lover, know; and I, the knower,
> Love—until both are saved.
>                                   (II.593–597)

Before he dies, Aprile desperately tries again to turn the thoughts of Paracelsus away from his fruitless endeavors by explaining that God, who is perfection, can best be seen in His own imperfect creations: "God is the PERFECT POET, / Who in his person acts his own creations" (II.610–611). But Paracelsus will not be content to seek God through imperfect means. Believing he has attained, he departs, intending to unite perfect knowledge and perfect love in his search for the secret of the universe.

CANTO THREE: "PARACELSUS"

We are introduced to a new side of Paracelsus' character in the third canto. Formerly, he has been either aspiring or attaining; now he has completely given up in his search for knowledge. Festus, who has come to Basel to visit the philosopher after a separation of nineteen years, is rather slow in penetrating Paracelsus' mask of indifference. Rumors of his friend's fame as a doctor and teacher have reached him in Würzburg, and he assumes that he has been successful in his undertaking. Through their conversation, Paracelsus' new attitudes toward love and knowledge, the basic themes of the poem, are revealed.

Mired in a state of bitter disillusionment, Paracelsus can face neither the present nor the future. He revels in the past and is offended when Festus reports that he and Michal now have children: "I detest all change, / And most a change in aught I loved long since" (III.49–50). Up to this time, Paracelsus had accepted change as àn indication that he was progressing in his search for knowledge. In Canto Two, he announced that through knowledge and the transformation wrought by knowledge he would become "The greatest and most glorious being on earth" (II.148). Now his attitude toward the value of becoming a knower is completely reversed. There is more to be wondered at in the simple, unsophisticated flowers of the earth than in the scant knowledge he has thus far managed to acquire:

> allowing I am passing wise,
> It seems to me much worthier argument
> Why pansies, eyes that laugh, are lovelier
> Than violets, eyes that dream . . .
> Than all fools find to wonder at in me,
> Or in my fortunes.
>
> (III.135–140)

Paracelsus mockingly informs Festus that the prophecy Michal offered in Canto One—"You will find all you seek, and perish so!" (I.732)—has not come true. In his bitterness, he seems to imply that Festus and Michal have no more claim to the power of prophecy (which, however, they never said they had) than he has to the power of obtaining knowledge:

> You were deceived, and thus were you deceived:
> I have not been successful, and yet am
> Most miserable.
>
> (III.270–272)

The further irony of the situation is that Paracelsus, even in his present despair, is closer to the truth than he has ever been before. In his former presumption, he proclaimed that he had direct access to knowledge of God's will. He boasts no longer:

> I know as much of any will of His
> As knows some dumb and tortur'd brute of what
> His stern lord wills from the bewildering blows
> That plague him every way.
>
> (III.543–546)

Moreover, whereas he had previously scorned partial truths in his search for knowledge, he now attempts to follow the counsel of Aprile, who advised him to subdue pride and "give my gains, imperfect as they were, / To men" (III.606–607). But, although he has consented to share his imperfect knowledge with the students at Basel, Paracelsus has not yet learned to control his pride. That "ready scorn" and "acquiescence in contempt" noticed by Festus in Canto One have not yet been cured. The students and fellow teachers at Basel are referred to by Paracelsus as "A tribe of wits" (III.226), "thick-scull'd youths" (III.159), "a gaping throng" (III.222), and "silly beardless boys, and bearded dotards" (III.438).

The truth is that Paracelsus does not accept his position at Basel as one which could lead to any positive attainment. He has failed in his original purpose, and remains at Basel only because he can see no alternative. Paracelsus tells Festus that he accepts this as his dull fate; his attitude is completely negative: "I plod on— / Subdued" (III.548–549). Festus knows Paracelsus too well to accept these words as the complete truth. When challenged by his friend to throw up his useless labor, Paracelsus confesses that he has not altogether lost sight of his original purpose, "to KNOW":

> My nature cannot lose her first impress;
> I still must hoard, and heap, and class all truths
> With one ulterior purpose—one intent.　　(III.737–739)

As Paracelsus describes his past endeavors to Festus, he reveals that he completely disregarded the argument of Aprile in Canto Two. Not only did he ignore the significance of Aprile's insistence on the incompleteness of man's vision, but he also failed to incorporate both love and knowledge into his quest. Instead, he made the same mistake Aprile himself had made: he tried "To live like that mad poet, for a while! / To love alone!" (III.728–729).

Even though his pursuit of both infinite knowledge and infinite love has thus far been unsuccessful, Paracelsus proposes to return "To courses void of hope" (III.800) in which he will continue to be "Sport for the gods" (III.804). This decision is a direct result of the shame he feels at accepting the unmerited praise of the crowds at Basel. He is acclaimed at Basel as a man of great knowledge only because he happened, by chance, to save the life of the ruling prince. Though he cannot soar to the heights he desires, he refuses to lower himself to the vanity of vulgar praise.

Festus, in an effort to encourage his friend, remarks that it is only human to be plagued by trials. Paracelsus scornfully replies that Festus' admiration blinds him to the truth. This elicits a statement on love by Festus which, since he has been so slow to understand the cause of Paracelsus' despair earlier in the canto, seems out of character. Because Festus' explanation contains the germinal answer to the problem of love as explained by Paracelsus in Canto Five, it becomes evident that Browning is here using Festus as his own mouthpiece:

> I say, such love is never blind; but rather
> Alive to every [sic] the minutest spot
> That mars its object, and which hate (supposed
> So vigilant and searching) dreams not of:
> Love broods on such: what then? In the first case
> Is there no sweet strife to forget, to change,
> To overflush those blemishes with all
> The glow of goodness they cannot disturb?

> To make those very defects an endless source
> Of new affection grown from hopes and fears?
>
> (III.877–886)

For Browning, love is not merely an aid in finding universal harmony; it is, rather, a power and a source of strength which makes harmony out of discord. It enables the beholder to see the smallest flaw in the object of love, and makes the flaws themselves a source of new affection. As Aprile stated before he died, it is only through acceptance of these flaws that man can ever hope to aspire to higher love and higher knowledge. Browning, through Festus, again stresses that the sin of Paracelsus lies in the denial of his own humanity. It springs "From one alone whose life has pass'd the bounds / Prescribed to life" (III.908–909).

Before Canto Three closes, Paracelsus tells Festus that his sufferings have not been completely without avail. He has, at least, learned that even if man were a pure intellectual being, "all mind," his position would hardly be enviable, for God and His "lowest spirit ministrant" would still possess an intelligence which would cast "*our* mind / Into immeasureable shade" (III.1089–1093). In addition, Paracelsus now understands what he has lost by cutting himself off from the rest of humanity:

> Love, hope, fear, faith—these make humanity;
> These are its sign, and note, and character;
> And these I have lost! gone; shut from me for ever.
>
> (III.1094–1096)

But Paracelsus still cannot apply any of these insights to his own plight. The reason for both his despair and his blindness is his inability to change his idea of what constitutes success. Absolute knowledge, which, paradoxically, he knows is impossible to achieve, remains Paracelsus' goal. Even at the close of Canto Three he insists that "Man must be fed / With angel's food" (III.1080–1081). In short, Paracelsus will not humble himself and admit his error in rejecting anything that is less than total perfection. Cantos Four and Five depict his capitulation to humility and his consequent success.

CANTO FOUR: "PARACELSUS ASPIRES"

Two years after his second meeting with Festus, Paracelsus again "aspires"; his aspirations, however, are those of a drunken cynic.

While speaking to Festus, Paracelsus reveals that the process of degradation begun in Canto Three is reaching its inevitable conclusion. He has been relieved of the lectureship at Basel and is now dependent upon "mantling wine" (IV.10) to help him face defeat. Although he tells Festus "Once more I aspire" (IV.47), it becomes clear that his aspirations are not identical to those discussed so many years before in the garden at Würzburg. Then Paracelsus was a proud, self-reliant seeker of truth; now he is a broken, dejected seeker of death.

In the first half of Canto Four, Paracelsus drunkenly explains that his dismissal from Basel does not constitute defeat, but that it has served to encourage him in his original aims. He tells Festus that there are four possible courses open to him. He can completely give up his former task and sink into a state of complete inactivity: "To shrink in like a crush'd snail—to endure / In silence and desist from further toil" (IV.162–163). Or, worse still, he could acquiesce to the wishes of those in power at Basel and "live as they prescribe, and make that use / Of all my knowledge which their rules allow" (IV.169–170). The only other choices are death or the renewal of his initial purpose, to know. The last alternative has been chosen, but Paracelsus is resolved to alter the means which are to help him acquire the desired prize:

> I will accept *all* helps; all I despised
> So rashly at the outset, equally
>
> . . . . . . . . . . .
>                             it shall not balk me
> Of the meanest, earthliest, sensualest delight
> That may be realized; for joy is gain,
> And gain is gain, however small.
>
>                             (IV.240–250)

And shortly after this declaration, Paracelsus announces his new attitude toward knowledge: "mind is nothing but disease, / And natural health is ignorance" (IV.282–283).

Although he admits to Festus that his words are the mere swaggerings of a defeated man who is attempting to "put a good face on the overthrow" (IV.322) he has experienced, these new attitudes toward love and knowledge are an important development in Paracelsus' final realization that his dreams of ethereal grandeur and mystic insight are purposeless. He no longer rejects all earthly pleasure, nor does he aspire to possess absolutes. Paracelsus now sees that his infinite goal is unattainable, and he understands that he must accept "All helps" even to gain the limited measure of love and knowledge which is within man's grasp. But, because of the extreme despair brought on by his sense of failure, he is unable to act on these discoveries.

That Paracelsus has learned something as a result of his trials at Basel becomes evident in a long lyric passage, described in the 1849 edition of the poem as a "parable," in which he relates to Festus a narrative of the journey and achievement of a group of seafarers. These men traveled to a desolate island, on which they built shrines in the rock to shelter a group of beautiful statues that had been found on board ship. When their task was completed, they learned that the island was uninhabited and that the people who had prepared to receive the statues lived on another island nearby. The meaning of the parable is clarified in the last few lines:

> we awoke with sudden start
> From our deep dream, and knew, too late,
> How bare the rock, how desolate,
> Which had received our precious freight:
> Yet we call'd out—"Depart!
> "Our gifts, once given, must here abide:
> "Our work is done; we have no heart
> "To mar our work," we cried.
>
> (IV.505–512)

Like the seafarers, Paracelsus began his quest in the blind ignorance which resulted from his initial idealism and impulsiveness. Like them, he refused to share his gift with mankind even when he fully comprehended the enormity of his error in isolating it. The statue (ideal knowledge) has been enshrined in the grotto of self-love, where it serves no other purpose than the glorification of its possessor. As Paracelsus states, the lyric is

> *"The sad rhyme of the men who proudly clung*
> *"To their first fault, and wither'd in their pride!"*
>
> (IV.517–518)

It seems, then, that Paracelsus does realize the futility of persisting in his original aims. He recognizes that pride in achievement has obscured his goal, which, as he stated in Canto One, was to serve mankind.

However, the problem of reconciling his will with the will of God still remains to be solved. Paracelsus believed in Canto One that he was directly appointed by God to become the sole savior of mankind. As long as he progressed in his search for knowledge, he continued to place his trust in God, but, in the despair of Canto Four, he claims that he no longer understands what God's will is. Festus now attempts to explain to Paracelsus that his major error has been in mistaking his own will for God's. In fact, Paracelsus has tried to make himself a God:

> So long
> As God would kindly pioneer your path—
> Would undertake to screen you from the world—
> . . . . . . . . . . . . .
> yield you
> A limitless license—make you God, in fact,
> And turn your slave—you were content to say
> Most courtly praises.
>
> (IV.558–566)

But Paracelsus clings with tenacity to the belief that God has failed him:

> I would have soothed my Lord, and slaved for him,
> And done him service past my narrow bond,
> And thus I get rewarded for my pains!
>
> (IV.590–592)

Thus shifting the blame for his failure to God, Paracelsus resolves to drown his sorrow in the narcotic joy of wine while waiting for death, "As though it matter'd how the farce plays out, / So it be quickly play'd" (IV.688–689).

CANTO FIVE: "PARACELSUS ATTAINS"

Paracelsus finally "attains" in Canto Five. For purposes of analysis, this canto, like the second one, can be divided into two parts. In the first section, Paracelsus, who is delirious, carries on an imagined conversation with Aprile in which he reviews the various hopes and failures he has experienced during a lifetime of searching. Festus, watching over the deathbed of his friend, begs for recognition during this state of delirium. When Paracelsus becomes conscious of his presence, the second section of the canto begins, and Paracelsus, in a moment of insight preceding death, reveals to Festus God's message— "God speaks to men through me!" (V.562). It is in this section of *Paracelsus* that the various ideas which Browning has been developing in the course of the poem are brought together to form a synthesis of the poet's thoughts about man and his relationship to God, and the nature of love and knowledge.

The canto opens on a positive note, indicating the general tone of what is to follow. As Festus sorrowfully observes the dying Paracelsus, he discusses God's justice in allowing such a supreme human being to fall to such a low state. Although he knows that Paracelsus has erred in placing a desire for his own glory above that of God, Festus believes that the salvation of such a man is still possible because the God of justice must also be a God of love and forgiveness:

> God! Thou art Love! I build my faith on that:
> Even as I watch beside thy tortured child,
> Unconscious whose hot tears fall fast by him,
> So doth thy right hand guide us through the world
> Wherein we stumble.
> . . . . . . . . . . . . .
> Save him, dear God; it will be like thee: bathe him
> In light and life!
>
> (V.50–66)

This affirmation of God as the God of love is consistent with Festus' position throughout the poem, both as the voice of Browning and in his own person; and it represents the pinnacle of the hierarchy of values Paracelsus has met with during the process of his discovery: the human love of Festus and Michal, the compassionate understanding of Festus, and the infinite aspiration to love of the poet Aprile. The importance of Festus' view is underlined when, later in Canto Five, Paracelsus accepts the value of human love because he sees it as a reflection of the divine love of God.

Browning has skillfully depicted the workings of a mind fatigued by toil and tortured by unfulfilled hopes in the rambling words of the delirious Paracelsus. The philosopher's first thought is of Aprile. He imagines that he and the poet are Promethean figures doomed to failure in their heroic endeavors by the curse of the gods:

> Ah, the curse, Aprile, Aprile!
> We get so near—so very, very near.
> 'Tis an old tale: Jove strikes the Titans down
> Not when they set about their mountain-piling,
> But when another rock would crown their work!
>
> (V.124–128)

Next, Paracelsus recalls his rejection from Basel, when he was scorned by his superiors as "The ignorant and incapable fool who thrust / Himself upon a work beyond his wits" (V.153–154). From thoughts of Basel, his mind wanders to one of the underlying causes of his failure, his withdrawal from human love. It has been noted that early in Canto Two, Paracelsus approached an understanding of his deficiency in love, but that the intrusion of Aprile hindered the carrying out of this realization to its logical conclusion. Again in Cantos Three and Four Paracelsus conversed with Festus, but his despair blinded him to the true value of what Festus represented. Now, unconsciously, Paracelsus discloses that the need of human love and his failure to grasp it have been more important causes of his lack of success than he has been willing to admit:

> your white limbs dazzled me. O white,
> And panting as they twinkled, wildly dancing!
> I cared not for your passionate gestures then,
> But now I have forgotten the charm of charms,
> While I remember that quaint dance;
>
> .  .  .  .  .  .  .  .  .  .  .  .  .
>
> I seek her now—I kneel—I shriek—
> I clasp her vesture—but she fades, still fades;
> And she is gone; sweet human love is gone!
>
> (V.187–205)

Finally, after reflecting on the complete futility of his life's search, "a poor cheat, a stupid bungle, / A wretched failure" (V.268–269), and briefly mentioning Aprile again, Paracelsus becomes aware of Festus' presence.

One positive indication that Paracelsus has not toiled in vain is his humble attitude toward knowledge and his fellow man:

> Dear Festus. I will kneel if you require me,
> Impart the meagre knowledge I possess,
> Explain its bounded nature, and avow

> My insufficiency—
>
> .  .  .  .  .  .  .  .  .  .  .  .
>
>                                       lay me
> When I shall die, within some narrow grave,
> Not by itself—for that would be too proud—
> But where such graves are thickest.
>
>                                       (V.349–359)

For the first time, Paracelsus is willing to admit without bitterness to Festus—and, more important, to himself—that his knowledge is "bounded" and that he is "insufficient." Whereas he once stated that he would have no contact with his fellow man, that he would not be served by those he serves, Paracelsus now wishes to take his place in the community of mankind, even if only in death.

Sensing that the end is near, and eager to communicate what "God speaks to men" through him, Paracelsus rises from the couch on which he is lying, dons his academic robe, and begins his final lecture. In Canto One, he visualized his life as an upward progress toward God, the culmination of which would add glory to God's power as well as praise and reverence to his own. He states in Canto Five that God's glory does not necessarily depend on perfection in the sphere of human activity, as he formerly believed, but that man, whether he is a success or failure, gives glory to God by his mere existence:

> We have to live alone to set forth well
> God's praise.
>
> .  .  .  .  .  .  .  .  .  .  .  .
>
>                              do your best
> Or worst, praise rises, and will rise for ever.
>
>                                       (V.576–580)

What Paracelsus has attained in his view of God is a new understanding of dependency—man depending on God rather than God on man. However, because God's glory is independent of man, this does not mean that He withdraws to a position of supremacy from which He looks down on man as a trivial play-toy. Instead, God is an absolute being who shares in the nature of all things and derives joy from the smallest, most insignificant of His creations:

> God tastes an infinite joy
> In infinite ways—one everlasting bliss,
> From whom all being emanates, all power

Proceeds; in whom is life for evermore,
Yet whom existence in its lowest form
Includes.

(V.654–659)

Paracelsus—and Browning—visualize God not only as a Being one must reach up to, but also as one whose presence must be recognized in His creations, whatever their place in the evolutionary scale of being:

He dwells in all,
From life's minute beginnings, up at last
To man—the consummation of this scheme
Of being—the completion of this sphere
Of life.

(V.692–696)

With his new conception of God and a new outlook on the value of created things, Paracelsus has simultaneously formed new attitudes toward love and knowledge. The knowledge that Paracelsus finally does attain is not the infinite knowledge which he had as his goal when he began his quest, nor does his definition of love bear any similarity to the infinite love of Aprile. In the four most important lines of the poem, Browning, through Paracelsus, states what love and knowledge must mean to man:

Knowledge: not intuition, but the slow
Uncertain fruit of an enhancing toil,
Strengthen'd by love—love: not serenely pure,
But power from weakness.

(V.709–712)

Absolutes are not accessible to man, who, in his finiteness, must be content with the "uncertain fruit" and the "toil" of limited knowledge and the "weakness" of human love. But even in this state of incompleteness there can be hope for improvement and desire for fulfillment. Man is not doomed to a nihilistic existence, "For all these things tend upward—progress is / The law of life" (V.755–756).

Browning's basic concerns, his ideas on progress, imperfection, human love, and human failure, all of which become thematic cornerstones in the dramatic monologues of the 1850's and 1860's, are presented and explained through Paracelsus' analysis of his own former lack of success in understanding the meaning of love:

In my own heart love had not been made wise
To trace love's faint beginnings in mankind—
To know even hate is but a mask of love's;
To see a good in evil, and a hope
In ill-success. To sympathize—be proud
Of their half-reasons, faint aspirings, struggles
Dimly for truth—their poorest fallacies,
And prejudice, and fears, and cares, and doubts;
All with a touch of nobleness, for all
Their error, all ambitious, upward tending,
Like plants in mines which never saw the sun,
But dream of him, and guess where he may be,
And do .their best to climb and get to him:
All this I knew not, and I fail'd.

(V.885–898)

And, with this acquisition of knowledge, the poem ends. Paracelsus attains the "secret of the world" in the acceptance of his own humanity, and Browning, by projecting his personal voice, experience, and ethical problems into the person of Paracelsus, answers some of the queries to which *Pauline* gave rise two years earlier.

Indeed, it is because Browning uses Paracelsus' career to work out a full statement of the problems which the hero of *Pauline* confronted, but defined much less clearly, that *Paracelsus* has been treated in such detail in this chapter. Both poems are concerned with resolving the dilemma which faces man: he must of necessity aspire, but he can never attain his goal. *Pauline* presents no satisfactory solution. Its hero can only grasp the flesh of Pauline's hand, move through material creation to a hope for better things, and pray to God, and Shelley, for aid. The resolutions presented in Paracelsus' final speech, which evolve out of the knowledge the philosopher has accumulated during his life, are much more incisive and persuasive.[12]

Through Paracelsus, the moral concerns which so troubled Browning in *Pauline* are presented, analyzed, and formulated into a series of

[12] Cf. F. E. L. Priestley's conclusion in "The Ironic Pattern of Browning's *Paracelsus*," *University of Toronto Quarterly*, XXXIV (October 1964), 81: "The true meaning is to be found only in the whole process." Priestley's essay deals with genre and irony in *Paracelsus* much more extensively than does my own work. But although this chapter was, for the most part, completed before Priestley's article appeared, my conclusions concerning the poem's meaning as a process of regenerative experience are similar to his.

poetic enunciations in Canto Five which, it must again be stressed, are meaningful only in terms of the total regenerative experience the poem depicts: infinites are unattainable to man in his present state of imperfection; imperfection, qualified by the necessity and inevitability of progress, is the law of life; progress, through imperfection, depends on the recognition that the flesh is not a "carnal mesh," but a temporal element which can contribute to man's ultimate perfection; and, finally, God rejoices and resides in all aspects of His creation, even to the extent of allowing man, in his weakness, to reflect His grandeur. These are the solutions arrived at by Browning in *Paracelsus* to his own fundamental problems, and they represent, in Raymond's words, "the basis" of the poet's "reflective thought on the fundamental problems of humanity."

## CHAPTER THREE

# *Sordello*: to Rifle a Musk-Pod

*Sordello* draws upon both *Pauline* and *Paracelsus* for its basic thematic structure. The first half of the poem depicts the central figure's poetic development in the isolation of Goito, and the second half concerns Sordello's attempt to enter the arena of public action when he moves from Goito to Mantua and then Ferrara. Like *Paracelsus*, *Sordello* is a poem in which Browning tries to gain objectivity in the analysis of his personal thoughts and feelings by projecting them into a historical figure.[1] Similarly, the central concern of each poem is reflected by the poet's particular choice of historical figures: through Paracelsus, the philosopher, Browning explores the moral questions raised by *Pauline* and indulges in a side glance at Shelley in the person of Aprile; through Sordello, the poet, he explores the aesthetic questions raised in *Pauline* and explains more fully the reasons for Aprile's failure in *Paracelsus*, placing particular emphasis on the nature of the poet and on the function of poetry as a mediating agent between the real and the ideal.

As explained in Chapter Two, Browning elucidates a number of theories in *Paracelsus* which can be comprehended with relative ease simply by following the hero of the poem in the process of his discovery. *Sordello* presents a much more perplexing problem to the student of Browning who wishes to read the poem as an exposition of his thought. It is not a very lucid work; there are a number of elements which contribute to its difficulty. To begin with, Browning treats more complex matters in greater detail than he did in either *Pauline* or *Paracelsus*. He is concerned with the artist as type, with the artist in society, with kinds of poetry and poetic experience, and with the manner in which Sordello responds to various pressures, both internal and external. Furthermore, the language of the poem is often

[1] E. D. H. Johnson, *The Alien Vision of Victorian Poetry* (Princeton: Princeton University Press, 1952), pp. 77–78.

incomprehensible, and the overlay of historical detail contributes little or nothing of interest to Sordello's story.

In addition, Browning presents this material in a much more disunified mixture of poetic forms than he used in either of his two previous long poems. *Pauline* is chaotic, but in the use of a single narrator, who is also the main subject of the poem, the reader is given some help in sorting out the confusion caused by the shifting of moods and chronological sequences. *Paracelsus* achieves clarity through dialogue and its approximation to the drama. *Sordello*, however, employs a number of forms—semidramatic, narrative, and expository flashback— which are alternated and juxtaposed by the narrator, who is Browning himself, with bewildering frequency.[2] But while *Sordello* is more confusing than either *Pauline* or *Paracelsus* because of its prolixity and the seemingly aimless mixing of poetic forms, the narrative base of the poem illustrates an important element in Browning's development. The shift from the total personal commitment of *Pauline* to the semidramatic manipulation of character in *Paracelsus* has already been noted as a positive advance. Browning does become more detached in *Paracelsus*, but even in this poem the detachment serves only to help him scrutinize his own problems; and Paracelsus' victory over the intellectual and emotional crises which he manufactures for himself also represents Browning's victory over the youthful moral crises depicted in *Pauline*. In *Sordello*, Browning is again using his hero to explore specific problems he himself faced, but in this case the poet is relatively free of his creation. The hero of *Sordello* is not a fictional substitute for Browning, although the phases of Sordello's career closely resemble those of the poet in *Pauline* and of Paracelsus. Through the use of the narrative mode, Browning is able to comment on the action as it happens—to enter the poem in his own voice and point out not only that Sordello fails both as a man and as a poet, but also why he fails. Sordello becomes a victim of aspiration rather than its hero, and

[2] Robert R. Columbus and Claudette Kemper, in "Sordello and the Speaker: A Problem in Identity," *Victorian Poetry*, II (Autumn 1964), 251–267, discuss the function of the "Speaker" in terms of *Sordello*'s rhetorical structure. Although their essay does serve to illuminate the structural role of the persona whose voice we hear throughout the poem, it tends to create an artificial distinction between the "Speaker" and Browning himself (see especially n. 2, p. 251). There is, however, as this chapter illustrates, little difference between the problems investigated by the "Speaker" of *Sordello* and the problems Browning was investigating during the period of the poem's composition.

Browning's ability to examine this character's career in light of his ultimate failure represents a stage of maturity one step removed from that apparent in *Paracelsus*.

Because of its technical flaws and its wide range of subject matter, *Sordello* has acquired the unhealthy critical reputation of being the most difficult long poem of the nineteenth century. The attitude of those who have read, or tried to read, the work is predominantly one of wry humor, and if these judgments are accepted, it becomes almost impossible to approach the poem seriously. William Macready, an early friend of Browning, assaulted the ramparts of *Sordello* a number of times and on July 17, 1840, made the following comment in his diary: "After dinner tried—another attempt—utterly desperate—on *Sordello*; it is *not* readable."[3] Harriet Martineau reacted just as extremely: "I was so wholly unable to understand it that I supposed myself ill."[4] Douglas Jerrold reportedly read *Sordello* when he was recovering from an illness and thought he was going mad; and Mrs. Carlyle is said to have read it through without being able to ascertain whether Sordello was a man, a book, or a city.[5] Finally, there is the comment by T. R. Lounsbury, which DeVane calls the "crowning pronouncement" upon the poem: "a colossal derelict upon the sea of literature, inflicting damage upon the strongest intellects that graze it even slightly, and hopelessly wrecking the frailer mental craft that come into full collision with it . . . ."[6] Despite the undeniable difficulty of *Sordello*, its chronological position in Browning's development and the nature of its subject matter warrant the effort to understand how these problems of composition arose and what it is that Browning is trying to say in the course of the poem's six long books.

There have been a number of noteworthy critical studies devoted to explaining the problems involved in *Sordello*'s impenetrability. Two articles by Stuart Walker Holmes approach *Sordello* from a psychological point of view. It is both interesting and suggestive to know that Browning "in his youth probably suffered from a case of unbalanced

[3] *The Diaries of William Charles Macready: 1833–51*, ed. William Toynbee (London: Chapman and Hall, 1912), II, 64.

[4] *Harriet Martineau's Autobiography*, ed. M. W. Chapman (Boston, 1877), I, 314.

[5] W. C. DeVane, *A Browning Handbook* (2d ed.; New York: Appleton-Century-Crofts, 1955), p. 85.

[6] *The Early Literary Career of Robert Browning* (New York: Charles Scribner's Sons, 1911), p. 92.

introversion"[7] and that when he "wrote as a prophet, as a meta-physician, he lost his ability to write meaningfully" because, being a "semantic stutterer," he "confused the levels of abstractions and dealt with the thing-word relationship intentionally rather than extensionally."[8] But such speculations tend to make a cloudy issue even more cloudy for the student unfamiliar with Jungian terminology. The work done by W. C. DeVane and Park Honan is more rewarding.

DeVane traces four different stages in the composition of *Sordello*, the first one beginning in 1833 and the last ending in 1839:

> The first of these was between March of 1833 and March 1st, 1834; that is, between the publication of *Pauline* and the beginning of Browning's trip to Russia. The second great period begins after the completion of *Paracelsus*, which was finished by March 15th, 1835, and continues until the end of February, 1836, when Forster's illness elicited Browning's aid for the *Life of Strafford*. Five months later Browning selected Strafford as the subject of his tragedy. The Strafford ventures are really episodes in the composition of *Sordello*, and properly the second great period of activity upon *Sordello* should not end in February, 1836, but should terminate with the publication of Mrs. Busk's *Sordello* on July 15th, 1837. The third period began about mid-September of 1837 and ended in mid-April of 1838, when Browning set sail for Italy. This, though not the longest of the periods, was probably the most feverish, and the trip to Italy was for the purpose of refreshing a jaded mind. The fourth period begins about August 1st, 1838, when Browning has returned to London, and when he has resolved to make an end of the work at all costs. It ends on May 26th, 1839, when Browning announces to his friends that *Sordello* is done.[9]

The result of this constant revision, each stage of which set the poem in a new thematic direction, is, as DeVane notes, a "conglomeration" of "psychology, love, romance, humanitarianism, philosophy and history...."[10] The most significant aspect of the revisions is that Browning, although probably exasperated by the necessity of shifting the emphasis of the poem so frequently, did so quite purposely. The

[7] "Browning's *Sordello* and Jung: Browning's *Sordello* in the Light of Jung's Theory of Types," *PMLA*, LVI (September 1941), 787.

[8] "Browning: Semantic Stutterer," *PMLA*, LX (March 1945), 231.

[9] "*Sordello*'s Story Retold," *Studies in Philology*, XXVII (January 1930), 12.

[10] *Ibid.*, p. 24.

same degree of conscious effort can be detected in his handling of the language in the poem.

Park Honan believes that *Sordello* is not so much the product of linguistic and prosodic experiments as it is "a considerable laboratory" [11] of experiments in itself. And I think it becomes clear, particularly in the introductory and concluding lines of the poem, that Browning was fully aware of the abstruseness caused by his attempt to experiment in the poetic laboratory. He has chosen the narrative method because he regards himself as one of those "Makers of quite new men" (I.28); [12] and, although he would rather keep himself out of sight and let Sordello speak for himself, he finds it advisable to "chalk broadly on each vesture's hem / The wearer's quality" (I.29–30). In the final lines of the poem he humorously chides those whom he knows will complain about *Sordello* because of its syntactical complications:

> any nose
> May ravage with impunity a rose—
> Rifle a musk-pod and 'twill ache like yours:
> I'd tell you that same pungency ensures
> An after-gust—but that were overbold.
>
> (VI.883–887)

Only if one accepts the primary assumption that Browning was fully aware of the thematic and stylistic difficulties which permeate *Sordello*, is it possible to consider the poem something other than a joke or a psychological oddity. Thus, working on the premise that *Sordello* must be taken seriously, and recognizing that its composition covers the most important years of Browning's formative period, particularly with regard to the various facets of aesthetic theory expressed in the poem, one may see that the "musk-pod" does contain some gusts which are worth rifling. And, indeed, only by literally rifling the poem, by catching at those elusive gusts which rise from the musk-pod without any consistent pattern or order, is it possible to comprehend the rich and varied complexity of *Sordello*'s subject matter.

[11] *Browning's Characters: A Study in Poetic Technique* (New Haven: Yale University Press, 1961), p. 37.

[12] Citations from *Sordello* are from the unnumbered text in Robert Browning's *Sordello* (London, 1840). Line numbers are added.

RECURRENT THEMES: ISOLATION, CENTRAL AIM, AND
COMPROMISE

Published in 1840 and extending in time of composition over the seven years immediately following the abortive publication of *Pauline*, *Sordello*, as is to be expected, contains certain elements of interest which Browning had partially exploited in *Pauline* and *Paracelsus*. Among them, there are three which are of major thematic importance, chiefly because in *Sordello*, centered on a poet figure, they are treated more fully and with greater relevance to Browning's own role as a poet than in either of his two previous works. In *Pauline* we are given the impression that the narrator's isolation from society and his inability to grasp and pursue a single course of action are detrimental to his function as a poet, but we are never allowed to form a very clear conception of how this isolation and vacillation affect the character's personality, nor, because he is the only figure in the poem, do we know how he measures up to the standards and achievements of other characters in his own world. In the same manner, we are led to understand in *Paracelsus* that the philosopher and the artist must make some compromise between reality and utopian ideals and that each must exercise his talent in and for society, but the discussion remains on a purely theoretical level; we do not learn the practical means by which Browning believed that compromise might be accomplished, although he definitely establishes that it is necessary. *Sordello*, by its inclusion of these themes—the dangers of isolation, the necessity for a central motivating goal tenaciously pursued, and the nature and manner of poetic compromise—may be said to represent the gathering and tying together of various strands of thought which Browning laid down in *Pauline* and *Paracelsus*.

Sordello's youthful training is not conducive to successful poetic endeavor, although at the outset of his career, he is described as a type of ideal poet physically and temperamentally:

> (The delicate nostril swerving wide and fine,
> A sharp and restless lip, so well combine
> With that calm brow) a soul fit to receive
> Delight at every sense.　　　　　　　　(I.469–472)

He spends his early years at Goito completely cut off from the business of the world, unable to remember having dwelt any other place, familiar with nothing outside the castle but the immediately adjoining woods, and limited in his knowledge of society to whatever he can glean from the gossip of the serving-women. The result of such isolation is, as noted in *Pauline*, indulgence in fancy and a tendency to attribute life to inanimate objects. In his "drowsy Paradise" (I.636), Sordello identifies with everything he sees, and each new discovery of incidental beauty brings added delight. Browning's central image in the first book of the poem, used to illustrate the narrowness of Sordello's world, is a font which the poet visits each day. It is supported by a group of marble statues in the form of maidens, some of whom stare at the ground with half-closed eyes, some of whom stand with arms crossed over their bosoms, and others who hide their eyes as if in shame. Around these maidens Sordello weaves his imaginative dreams, and they become, for him, exiled priestesses for whom his role is to pray, to beg "Pardon for them" (I.435):

> So dwell these noiseless girls, patient to see,
> Like priestesses because of sin impure
> Penanced for ever, who resigned endure,
> Having that once drunk sweetness to the dregs.
>
> (I.430–433)

As he matures, Sordello begins to feel a vague dissatisfaction in meditating on the attributes of others while lacking an understanding of his own individuality and personality. Gradually, gaining some insight into the true nature of objects outside of himself, he

> managed rip
> Their fringe off, learn the true relationship,
> Core with its crust, their natures with his own,
>
> (I.715–717)

and at the same time he begins to feel the need of "some special office" (I.735) through which he can parade his greatness before mankind. Browning here interjects a comment which illuminates his attitude toward the condition which inevitably accompanies the turning of a poet's interest inward to himself. Such poetic types practice their art and seek the company of men only because they need the assurance that what they claim for themselves is justified by the opinion of others. Souls like Sordello

> Coerced and put to shame, retaining Will,
> Care little, take mysterious comfort still,
> But look forth tremblingly to ascertain
> If others judge their claims not urged in vain
> —Will say for them their stifled thoughts aloud;
> So they must ever live before a crowd.

> (I.760–765)

Sordello's immediate problem is how to draw men's attention to himself. He resolves to integrate all the best qualities of other men into his own personality. In this way, his composite being would become a mirror in which men could identify their own best selves, and during this process of recognition, they would also become aware of the poet's greatness. Thinking that perhaps he might even excel the heroes of the world whom he imitates, Sordello imagines himself dressed in the guise of a famous warrior and tries to lift a heavy sword. Although he fails even in this, he convinces himself that some day a means will be found to express his ideal. Sordello believes that, given time, his soul will find a body, an instrument, through which he will be able to act out all his fantastic desires:

> though I must abide
> With dreams now, I may find a thorough vent
> For all myself, acquire an instrument
> For acting what these people act; my soul
> Hunting a body out, obtain its whole
> Desire some day!

> (I.857–862)

For the present he is content, like the hero of *Pauline*, who resolves to emulate the "Sun-treader," and Paracelsus, who sees himself as a knight traversing a wilderness, to imagine that he is Apollo, a being of perfect attributes who is superior to the rest of mankind.

Shortly after, Sordello wanders into Mantua and encounters the crowd gathered to hear Eglamor, Palma's famous minstrel, sing. Listening, Sordello becomes extremely excited, for he sees that Eglamor, in his enthusiasm, is leaving the song incomplete and that he, hitherto inexperienced in public performance, can supply the gaps. Completely forgetting the selfish desires nurtured at Goito, he sings for the sake of the song itself and what it communicates to the people, rather than for the adulation which he may receive:

Sordello's brain
Swam; for he knew a sometime deed again;
So could supply each foolish gap and chasm
The minstrel left in his enthusiasm,
Mistaking its true version.

(II.74–78)

Vanquishing Eglamor, who dies as a result of his defeat, Sordello becomes Palma's minstrel and is given a chance to realize his high ambitions. However, this goal is frustrated, for he soon becomes dissatisfied with the lack of recognition afforded him by an unappreciative public. He returns to Goito for sanctuary and the peace of isolation, just as the poet of *Pauline* contemplates the possibility of escape into seclusion following his disillusionment, and as Paracelsus allows himself to indulge in lonely self-pity after being ousted from Basel. Later, when he is summoned to aid Palma with a plot involving the overthrow of the Guelphs by the Ghibellines, Sordello wavers irresolutely trying to decide the exact role he should play. This is his opportunity to win the admiration of men and make a decision which could aid society, but because he has been nourished on fancy and has grown to manhood surrounded by the "drowsy Paradise" of Goito, he is totally unprepared to meet the demands of a practical situation which requires a thorough understanding of self, and of reality.

Sordello's lack of resolution and his inability to give his life any significant purpose is dwelt on by Browning throughout the poem, and it is most effectively illustrated by the frequent comparisons between Sordello and other members of his own society. Eglamor, the defeated poet, is not a great artist and does not possess Sordello's potentiality for success, but his superiority to the Sordello we see in the early books of the poem is evident. His poetry is representative of his best efforts, and his achievement is therefore a valuable one in Browning's estimation:

note
In just such songs as Eglamor, say, wrote
With heart and soul and strength, for he believed
Himself achieving all to be achieved
By singer—in such songs you find alone
Completeness.

(III.622–627)

Similarly, Palma is superior to Sordello because she is willing to take positive action in order to end the political strife between the Guelphs and the Ghibellines from which Sordello retreats.

The most direct contrast which throws into relief Sordello's inability to pursue a central aim is that explicitly set up by Browning between Sordello and his father, Salinguerra—between the irresolute poet weakened by selfishness and ignorance of the real world, and the soldier who is a man of action. The difference between the two men, rendered even more incongruous by their blood relationship, is reflected in their physical appearances. Sordello is an old man before his time, and he has accomplished nothing:

> that minstrel's thirty autumns spent
> In doing nought, his notablest event
> This morning's journey hither . . .
> Who yet was lean, outworn and really old,
> A stammering awkward youth.
>
> (IV.415–419)

Salinguerra, on the other hand, has in his sixty years undergone varied experiences, risen to the position of a leader, and, most important, is selflessly dedicated to the military life. Yet he remains "agile quick / And graceful" (IV.426–427), and, within his limited scope of endeavor, puts Sordello to shame:

> his life
> Suffered its many turns of peace and strife
> In many lands—you hardly could surprise
> A man who shamed Sordello (recognise)
> In this as much beside, that, unconcerned
> What qualities are natural or earned,
> With no ideal of graces, as they came
> He took them, singularly well the same.
>
> (IV.576–583)

The difference between the two men is further emphasized by their varying approaches to the public. Salinguerra seeks knowledge of men because he is interested in judging their characters and determining whether their motives are compatible with his own; Sordello seeks knowledge of men solely for the purpose of discovering how they can contribute to his own vanity:

> Taurello [Salinguerra], ever on the watch
> For men, to read their hearts and thereby catch
> Their capabilities and purposes,
> Displayed himself so far as displayed these:
> While our Sordello only cared to know
> About men as a means for him to show
> Himself, and men were much or little worth
> According as they kept in or drew forth
> That self.
>
> (IV.600–608)

Browning's depiction of Sordello's total inadequacy in facing his early crises (his frustration at being unable to please the crowd, his refusal to celebrate Salinguerra's arrival at Mantua, his withdrawal to Goito, and his indecision concerning a course of action) is closely allied thematically and, possibly, in time of composition to his treatment of Aprile in *Paracelsus* and, consequently, to his mistrust of the Apollo-like aspirations of Shelley, or of any poet who is committed to an idealistic conception of the artist's role. Browning believed that there must be some compromise between an individual's aspirations and the actual possibilities for action—whether it be in the poetic, philosophic, military, or any other field of human activity—which can be undertaken with the hope of fruitful results. *Sordello*, even more completely than *Paracelsus*, explains the terms within which this compromise must be effected. While Paracelsus understands the necessity of limited aspirations and the value of seeking imperfection, Sordello is led to understand how this compromise affects the individual personality and society. Although Browning delves more deeply into this subject in *Sordello*, it should be stressed that the same principles serve as the basis for the thematic development of both poems; and while it is true that one poem is chiefly devoted to moral and the other to aesthetic values, the distinction between these two areas of thought is, for Browning, a very slight one.

Sordello touches on the nature of the reconciliation between aspiration and possible achievement early in Book Three, when he returns to Goito to consider the reasons for his failure at Mantua. He regretfully acknowledges that his idealistic conceptions, formulated in the mind and essentially independent of reality, must be tempered by an acceptance that even he is, after all, only a man:

> I must, ere I begin to Be,
> Include a world, in flesh, I comprehend
> In spirit now.
>
> (III.174–176)

The soul of man is insufficient in itself because, whatever its powers, it has no independently functioning organs. An Apollo figure is interesting to contemplate; but for a person who can hardly lift a sword, the pretensions of being an Apollo are more than slightly absurd:

> he found
> Not only that a soul, howe'er its might,
> Is insufficient to its own delight
> Both in corporeal organs and in skill
> By means of such to body forth its Will—
> And, after, insufficient to apprise
> Men of that Will, oblige them recognise
> The Hid by the Revealed.
>
> (III.564–571)

Up to this point, Sordello has learned that his poetic ambitions can never be completely realized because of the restrictive nature of the body through which his soul must work. But rather than acting upon this knowledge by attempting to fit his own soul to his own body, Sordello deludes himself into thinking that he could still achieve the full potentiality of his powers if he were to acquire a new body—one which would more adequately conform to the immensity of his infinite aspirations. The body he will use is that of mankind itself: "With his own will, effect a happiness / From theirs, supply a body to his soul" (IV.205–206). But this new instrument must be perfect, so Sordello decides that his initial task should be to reform the masses, to "think of men and of their wants," and then he will be able to use them to complete himself: "after that, of wondrous qualities / Of his own soul demanding exercise" (IV.269–273). Thus in the second half of the poem, Sordello's primary aim is centered on social rather than poetic action. Like Paracelsus, who strives to attain both infinite love and infinite knowledge after his meeting with Aprile, Sordello shifts the direction of his error but does not correct it. He still must learn that compromise is necessary in any form of human endeavor.

Accompanied by Palma, Sordello travels to Ferrara to visit Salinguerra and discover the means by which society might be perfected. However, Salinguerra's practical political concerns clash with Sordello's idealistic aims. The interview is short and discouraging for the would-be leader of mankind:

> Scarcely an hour past
> When forth Sordello came, older by years
> Than at his entry.
>
> (IV.334–336)

Still Sordello persists. Rather than becoming involved in the strife between the Guelphs and the Ghibellines, he now convinces himself that there must be a third and nobler cause which will encompass the other two. In order to put mankind "Once more in full possession of their rights / By his sole agency" (IV.1012–1013), Sordello resolves "To build up Rome again" (IV.1014). This plan lasts for only one day; he can find no shining citizens for his ideal city:

> Are this and this and this the shining ones
> Meet for the Shining City? Sooth to say
> Our favoured tenantry pursue their way
> After a fashion! This companion slips
> On the smooth causey, t'other blinkard trips
> At his mooned sandal. Leave to lead the brawls
> Here i'the atria? No, friend. He that sprawls
> On aught but a stibadium suffers . . . goose,
> Puttest our lustral vase to such an use?
> Oh, huddle up the day's disasters—march
> Ye runagates, and drop thou, arch by arch,
> Rome!
>
> (V.9–20)

Sordello's plan to create a new Rome through instant social revolution parallels, in its weakness, his earlier plan to accomplish the impossible through poetry. Like the hero of *Pauline* and Paracelsus, he would overleap the bounds of reality. Browning, in narrative voice, intrudes to explain that any plan of development must be a gradual step-by-step process which takes into consideration both the limitations of the workman and the attendant temporal circumstances. His advice echoes the evolutionary theory stated in the final canto of *Paracelsus*:

> Rest thy wit
> And listen: step by step,—a workman fit
> With each, nor too fit,—to one's task, one's time,—
> No leaping o'er the petty to the prime,
>
> .   .   .   .   .   .   .   .   .   .   .
>
> Better (say you) merge
> At once all workmen in the demiurge,
> All epochs in a life-time, and all tasks
> In one.
>
> (V.49–62)

But, unlike Paracelsus, Sordello will not learn the lesson of experience. He returns to Salinguerra, this time in an attempt to persuade the soldier to desert the Ghibellines and become the leader of the Guelph cause. Salinguerra, however, shifts the responsibility of decision to Sordello by throwing the badge of Ghibelline authority over his shoulders. Once again Sordello is caught in a dilemma: Should he accept the badge, become the Ghibelline leader, take his rightful place as Salinguerra's son, and wed Palma; or should he renounce all in favor of the Guelphs, who, he is firmly convinced, represent the interests of the people? The burden of decision is too much for him to bear. When Palma and Salinguerra return to the room in which they left Sordello to ponder the question, they find the poet-reformer dead, with the badge crushed under his foot. And although Palma thinks she detects "A triumph lingering in the wide eyes" (VI.618), Browning implies that even if Sordello did make a decision, it is, after all, of little consequence. Of what value is any decision if man cannot face life itself:

> —As one content to merely be supposed
> Singing or fighting elsewhere, while he dozed
> Really at home—and who was chiefly glad
> To have achieved the few real deeds he had
> Because that way assured they were not worth
> Doing, so spared from doing them henceforth—
>
> .   .   .   .   .   .   .   .   .   .   .   .
>
> a sorry farce
> Such life is after all.
>
> (VI.841–853)

Sordello ends his life literally plagued to death by his blindness to the necessity of tempering ambition, whether it be poetic or social, with the compromise demanded by reality.

An additional reason for Sordello's failure is presented in the sixth book of the poem, in an analysis given partly by Sordello himself as he surveys his wasted life, and partly by Browning, who steps in to supply the answers Sordello cannot find. The soul, or the spiritual faculty of man, is joined to matter, or the body, and must adjust to its temporal circumstances or, in its failure to accomplish its ends, bring about sorrow and disharmony:

> Soul on Matter being thrust,
> 'Tis Joy when so much Soul is wreaked in Time
> On Matter,—let the Soul attempt sublime
> Matter beyond its scheme and so prevent
> Or more or less that deed's accomplishment,
> And Sorrow follows: Sorrow to avoid—
> Let the Employer match the thing Employed,
> Fit to the finite his infinity,
>
> .    .    .    .    .    .    .    .    .    .    .
> 
>          limited
> To the appointed circumstance and dead
> To all beyond.
>
>         (VI.494–505)

In Sordello's particular case, this reconciliation had not taken place. Soul had outrun the body and tried to force it to accomplish what it was not equipped to do; hence the body had slowly degenerated, and Sordello at thirty years of age looked older than Salinguerra did at sixty:

> the poor Body soon
> Sinks under what was meant a wondrous boon,
> Leaving its bright accomplice all aghast.
>
>         (VI.549–551)

However, to understand the problem is not to find a positive solution, and Sordello's immediate query is a practical one. How does man "so order Life" (VI.575)? The common method, that of the "sad world," is to "brutalize / The soul" by muffling all sensibility (VI.575–578), and this is obviously not the answer. Here Browning interrupts—"Ah my Sordello, I this once befriend / And speak for you" (VI.592–593)— and offers an explanation which throws considerable light not only on the potential love relationship between Sordello and Palma, but also on Browning's idea of what motivates true human love. Man, says Browning, desperately requires belief in a divine being, the nature of whom, though far beyond his comprehension, is worthy of devotion and love:

> A Power above him still
> Which, utterly incomprehensible,
> Is out of rivalry, which thus he can
> Love, tho' unloving all conceived by Man—
> What need!　　　　　　　　　　　(VI.593–597)

And to make this love fruitful, it must be completed by something else. The poet should not seek a method of direct access to this divine power, nor should he desire a knowledge of it which would instill in him a desire for the same degree of greatness. He must establish a relationship with a human being who, for him alone, would represent the divinity on earth. This person, knowing the divinity's will, would direct him in the path already chosen by that "out-Nature":

> And of—none the minutest duct
> To that out-Nature, nought that would instruct
> And so let rivalry begin to live—
> But of a Power its representative
> Who, being for authority the same,
> Communication different, should claim
> A course the first chose and this last revealed—
> This Human clear, as that Divine concealed—
> The utter need!　　　　　　　　　　　(VI.597–605)

For Sordello, that human being is Palma.[13] From her he might have

---

[13] Browning calls this type of individual an "out-soul" (III.314). Elsewhere in the poem, it is suggested that a person who fills this capacity acts as a source of inspiration for the poet, and that the relationship is based on love. Lack of both inspiration and love contributed to Sordello's failure:

> Demanding only outward influence,
> A soul, in Palma's phrase, above his soul,
> Power to uplift his power, this moon's control,
> Over the sea-depths
> ·　·　·　·　·　·　·　·　·
> 　　　　　but years and years the sky above
> Held none, and so, untasked of any love,
> His sensitiveness idled.　　　　　　　(VI.41–48)

learned before it was too late that his role as a poet in society was not to pick up sword and cudgel and, through physical coercion, persuade men of the superior merit of either the Guelph or the Ghibelline cause. Rather, he should have employed song to produce action in others. This is one important purpose of the poet in society:

> producing deeds but not by deeds,
> Swaying, in others, frames itself exceeds,
> Assigning them the simpler tasks it used
> As patiently perform till Song produced
> Acts.

(V.554–558)

The sorrow of Sordello's life is that because of his youthful self-deception, his inability to pursue a clearly defined goal, and his unwillingness to recognize the necessity of compromise, his potential role as a poet in society remained unfulfilled.

### OF POETS AND POETRY

*Sordello* sinks into obscurity in many places, but there is at least one important compensation for the numerous lines which mean nothing even after the most strenuous wrenching of syntax and reordering of words. Buried beneath the historical detail and the long passages in which Sordello, Salinguerra, and Palma reflectively explore their pasts and their plans for the resolution of the civil strife between the forces of Rome and those of Frederick II, Browning can sometimes be heard speaking out on various theoretical problems. In this respect *Sordello* is unique among Browning's early poems, and his recognition of its uniqueness is indicated in the opening lines of the poem in which he explains the reasons for his use of the narrative method. The most important and interesting of these theoretical diversions are the ones in which Browning distinguishes between and evaluates various types of poets and poetic endeavor.

These, however, cannot be treated, as can those recurrent themes discussed above, solely in terms of Sordello's career. For although Browning's reflections on the poet and the nature of poetry do occur in the poem and are suggested by the plot, they are not positively stated or resolved in terms of the plot. In his discussion of the role of the poet, Browning explains that the true poet can never accomplish what he desires in this grimy, imperfect society; he must not only find beauty in the ugly, the whole in the broken, but he must also be content to accomplish partial good. Similarly, poetry itself can never be perfect; at best it will be an inadequate verbal instrument which only partially expresses the total poetic vision. Sordello as hero fails to grasp clearly either one of these principles. He is broken, rather than usefully changed or educated, by his attempt to bypass these restrictions on both the poet and his poetry. But Browning is clear about these ideas; and through his use of the narrative mode, he focuses the reader's attention, even more clearly than he did in *Paracelsus*, on his belief that man has to pursue the infinite, even though it is inaccessible. And man must pursue it in Browning's, not Sordello's, way—in patient and partial celebration of the always incomplete and ultimately disappointing finite. While Browning obliquely suggests these principles through his depiction of Sordello's failure to actively comprehend them, he delineates them clearly in the frequent, though dispersed, theoretical statements which are examined in the following pages.

Browning accepted the commonly held belief that the poet is a man set apart from those less sensitive than himself, and that his major advantage lies in the perception of beauty. He is one of the "regal class" (I.473) in whom we

> recognise at once the finer dress
> Of flesh that amply lets in loveliness
> At eye and ear, while round the rest is furled
>
> · · · · · · · · · · · ·
>
> A veil that shows a sky not near so blue,
> And lets but half the sun look fervid through.
>
> (I.483–488)

Within this "regal class" there are those who take different approaches to beauty, to the matter of integrating poetry and the personality of the poet, and to the problem of exactly what the poet must do in his art in order to achieve the goal of initiating action in other men.

Browning seems to think that the true poet must progress through a number of stages before he reaches a valid perception of beauty, and that his ultimate success depends on his ability to merge his own being with the object of contemplation. The scale of ascendency toward the highest level of perception begins with the discovery of beauty and delight in it for its own sake, "blind at first to aught / Beyond its beauty" (I.490–491). Such momentary joy is, however, quickly satiated, and the poet then begins to endow the object with qualities of his own being—"invest / The lifeless thing with life from their own soul" (I.496–497)—until he is moved by the desire to employ his special insight for a purpose outside of self: "employ / That beauty fitly, for its proper sake" (I.500–501). Finally, the poet comes to understand how the individual objects of beauty fit into a larger scheme; the various aspects of beauty are seen as a unity which expresses the sum of all beauty, God:

> every grade of love is past,
> With every mode of loveliness; then cast
> Inferior idols off their borrowed crown
> Before a coming glory: up and down
> Runs arrowy fire, while earthly forms combine
> To throb the secret forth; a touch divine—
> And the scaled eyeball owns the mystic rod:
> Visibly through his garden walketh God.
>
> (I.503–510)

To become such a poet, it is absolutely necessary for the individual to suppress self:

> one character
> Denotes them through the progress and the stir;
> A need to blend with each external charm,
> Bury themselves, the whole heart wide and warm,
> In something not themselves; they would belong
> To what they worship.
>
> (I.511–516)

At the other extreme we have poets like Sordello, the hero of *Pauline*, Aprile, and the Robert Browning of the 1830's. Because he spends so much more verbal energy dissecting this type of poet than any other, striving to understand what motivates such a man, Browning seems to be attempting to comprehend the causes of poetic failure so that he can acquire the knowledge to change the direction in which he feels he himself is drifting. Each of these poet figures, including Browning, has "the mark / Of leprosy upon him, violet dark" (I.575–576).

The leper poet, eaten away by the gnawing canker of self-love, regards the beauty he sees as a reflection or a double of what he already possesses in himself. Any new acquisition of beauty is regarded as an instinct nurtured in his own soul which, previously indistinct, is now remembered and recognized as his own creation:

> each new revealment born a twin
> With a distinctest consciousness within
> Referring still the quality, now first
> Revealed, to their own soul; its instinct nursed
> In silence, now remembered better, shown
> More thoroughly, but not the less their own.
>
> (I.531–536)

The true artist pays tribute to God by acknowledging Him as the sum of all beauty; the false artist, like the false philosopher, adores self: "homage other souls direct / Without, turns inward" (I.541–542). And although the extremities of self-consciousness disallow meaningful poetic expression, these poets have the dubious consolation of living completely unto themselves, and they possess the ability to soar in imagination from the lowest form of individual life to a deluded understanding of the most complex heavenly being:

> laugh thou at envious fate,
> Who from earth's simplest combination stampt
> With individuality—uncrampt
> By living its faint elemental life,
> Dost soar to heaven's complexest essence, rife
> With grandeurs, unaffronted to the last,
> Equal to being all.
>
> (I.548–554)

When the overly egocentric and hyperimaginative poet turns his attention to mankind, there are two alternatives open to him, one of which is just as useless as the other, and both of which Browning discusses with a penetration that reveals the personal knowledge gained through his analysis of similar alternatives in *Pauline* and *Paracelsus*. He either rejects his opportunity to answer the needs of mankind because this course would be considered stooping into a sphere of activity which would contribute nothing to his conception of self,

> (Too narrow an arena to reward
> Emprize—the world's occasion worthless since
> Not absolutely fitted to evince
> Its mastery).
>
> (I.566–569)

Or, even worse, he tries to display in this life a completeness of vision and mastery of purpose which can only be fulfilled in another life:

> a desire possess it to put all
> That nature forth, forcing our straitened sphere
> Contain it; to display completely here
> The mastery another life should learn,
> Thrusting in time eternity's concern.
>
> (I.570–574)

Finally, the question arises as to how the impersonal poet, who has successfully learned to appreciate beauty, communicates his knowledge to other men for the purpose of "producing deeds but not by deeds" (V.554). Browning states that the office of the poet is primarily dedicated to the observation of his fellow man, and he differentiates among three ways in which the poet employs his observations in the composition of poetry. The first and least effective method is simply to repeat, descriptively, what has been seen. The second and somewhat more valuable method is to add a short commentary and explain how the subject appeared to the poet. The third and highest level of communication enables common man to see with the eyes of the poet. The insight this kind of poet possesses is particularly valuable, for he has the unique ability of seeing into the very essence of another man by reading what is disclosed on his face:

> The office of ourselves nor blind nor dumb
> And seeing somewhat of man's state, has been,
> The worst of us, to say they so have seen;
> The better, what it was they saw; the best,
> Impart the gift of seeing to the rest:
> So that I glance, says such an one, around,
> And there's no face but I can read profound
> Disclosures in; this stands for hope, that—fear.
>
> (III.862–869)

One of the elements which the poet tries to detect, and in turn to integrate into his poetry, is the mood which engulfs the subject, and the causes underlying that mood:

> 'Tis of the mood itself I speak, what tinge
> Determines it, else colourless, or mirth,
> Or melancholy, as from Heaven or Earth.
>
> (III.908–910)

Having made these distinctions between poets, Browning next contrasts poets and other men of special talent. The trouble with all poets is, he laments, their inability to turn their talent for observation to its greatest advantage because, as a race, they are utterly incapable of action. For this reason he admits that the "crowd" may be right in allowing more praise to fall on the Salinguerras of the world than on the Sordellos:

> Not so unwisely hastes the crowd dispense
> On Salinguerras praise in preference
> To the Sordellos: men of action these!
> Who seeing just as little as you please
> Yet turn that little to account.
>
> (III.917–921)

With a rare show of humor he then explains that the time when the true poet also becomes a man of action will not be in this life:

> In short,
> When at some future no-time a brave band
> Sees, using what it sees, then shake my hand
> In heaven, my brother!
>
> (III.924–927)

Nevertheless, talented poets should be kept at their tasks, since they do have an important function to perform and other men would feel their absence if they gave up their work:

> Meanwhile where's the hurt
> To keep the Makers-see on the alert
> At whose defection mortals stare aghast
> As though Heaven's bounteous windows were slammed
> Incontinent?
>
> (III.927–931)

In the fifth book of *Sordello*, Browning, through a classification and evaluation of genres, again turns to a consideration of the manner in which poets express their insights.[14] Within the hierarchy of genres, his basis of evaluation depends upon the facility with which the poet is able to lead the reader into a direct participation in the life of the poem, the extent to which the poet is able to disengage himself from the work, and the degree of the author's insight into the nature of the characters with whom he is dealing.[15]

The epic is, in Browning's analysis, the least valuable of poetic forms, because its meaning depends wholly on the emphasis the poet chooses to place on the subjects involved. The reader can only listen and accept without question the poet's interpretation:

> marshal yon Life's elemental Masque
> Of Men, on evil or on good lay stress,
> This light, this shade make prominent, suppress
> All ordinary hues that softening blend
> Such natures with the level: apprehend
> Which evil is, which good, if I allot
> Your Hell, the Purgatory.
>
> .  .  .  .  .  .  .  .  .  .
>
> These fail to recognise, to arbitrate
> Between henceforth, to rightly estimate
> Thus marshalled in the Masque! Myself, the while,
> As one of you, am witness, shrink or smile
> At my own showing!
>
> (V.567–584)

Next highest in order of value is the drama. In this mode the characters are freer to act out their own roles, the poet retires to a position similar to that of a puppetmaster, and the emphasis of the work is directed to the revelation of moral qualities, with little emphasis on external action:

---

[14] Although these ideas are presented as the reported speech of Sordello, their clarity, as well as their relationship to Browning's mature poetic technique, would seem to justify a discussion of them as reflective of Browning's own mind. The same conclusion, based on a different premise, is reached by Daniel Stempel in "Browning's *Sordello*: The Art of the Makers-See," *PMLA*, LXXX (December 1965), 559.

[15] Browning may also intend this to be a historical discussion of genres. Whether he does or not makes little difference, since the essential aspect of his treatment is evaluative. See V.603–607.

> The men and women stationed hitherto
> Will I unstation, good and bad, conduct
> Each nature to its farthest or obstruct
> At soonest in the world: Light, thwarted, breaks
> A limpid purity to rainbow flakes,
> Or Shadow, helped, freezes to gloom: behold
> How such, with fit assistance to unfold,
> Or obstacles to crush them, disengage
> Their forms, love, hate, hope, fear, peace make, war wage,
> In presence of you all!
>
> (V.585–594)

The third genre, one in which the poet can "unveil the last of mysteries" (V.599), is synthetic poetry, but unfortunately, Browning is not willing to discuss this kind of poetry at any great length, perhaps because he feels it should be self-evident that *Sordello* is an attempt to write in this genre.[16] He does state, however, that such poetry is devoid of "externals" (probably meaning physical action), that it exposes man's inner nature more completely than either the epic or the drama, and that the reader enters more fully into the work:

> Man's life shall have yet freer play:
> Once more I cast external things away
> And Natures, varied now, so decompose
> That . . . but enough! Why fancy how I rose,
> Or rather you advanced since evermore
> Yourselves effect what I was fain before
> Effect, what I supplied yourselves suggest,
> What I leave bare yourselves can now invest?
>
> (V.600–607)

The way the reader is to be drawn into the work is through its style:

> Why fancy . . .
> .   .   .   .   .   .   .   .   .   .   .
> How we attained tò talk as brothers talk,
> In half-words, call things by half-names, no balk

[16] In the 1863 Preface to *Sordello*, dedicated to J. Milsand, Browning does suggest, in more specific terms, that he thinks the value of *Sordello* lies in its synthetic nature: "The historical decoration was purposely of no more importance than a background requires; and my stress lay on the incidents in the development of a soul: little else is worth study" (DeVane, *Handbook*, p. 73). The terms used in my text to describe the genres are derived from the page headings added by Browning in the 1863 edition, i.e., "epoist," "dramatist," and "synthetist."

From discontinuing old aids—To-day
Takes in account the work of Yesterday—
Has not the world a Past now, its adept
Consults ere he dispense with or accept
New aids?

.  .  .  .  .  .  .  .  .  .  .

           leave the mere rude
Explicit details, 'tis but brother's speech
We need, speech where an accent's change gives each
The other's soul—no speech to understand
By former audience—need was then expand,
Expatiate—hardly were they brothers! true—
Nor I lament my less remove from you,
Nor reconstruct what stands already:

.  .  .  .  .  .  .  .  .  .

          my art intends
New structure from the ancient.      (V.603–626)

"Brother's speech" is poetry in which there exists such a close rapport between the mind of the poet and his listener that it is possible to achieve the transference of thought from one person to the other by nuances of intonation, vague suggestion, and the association of apparently unrelated ideas. Nothing is explained in detail, and where history supplies a meaning there is no necessity of explicating the subject again. Formerly, men were required to "expatiate" or expand their ideas in order to communicate with each other. Now it should be possible to attain maximum communication with a minimum indulgence in language.

However, Browning, having learned his lesson well, probably in the composition of *Sordello*, is quite aware that the same gulf which separates aspiration from the possibility of achievement with respect to life itself separates an ideal theory of poetry from the technical realities which the practice of poetry demands. Synthetic poetry, couched in "brother's speech," is in theory the highest level of poetic achievement, but Browning knows that language will never be an adequate instrument to accomplish the ends poetry sets for itself. Just as the potentiality of the soul is limited by the body, the poet's desire to communicate is limited by words:

Ah, whose that fortune? ne'ertheless
E'en he must stoop contented to express

> No tithe of what's to say—the vehicle
> Never sufficient.
>
> (V.634–637)

For a concrete example of what does take place when a poet tries to make language do too much, and the reasons for its ultimate inadequacy, we must turn to Sordello's experiment in Book Two. He manipulates his language and recasts his style in order to allow himself more complete expression:

> he sought
> The cause, conceived a cure, and slow re-wrought
> That Language, welding words into the crude
> Mass from the new speech round him, till a rude
> Armour was hammered out.
>
> (II.586–590)

But the armor falls to pieces because whole or complete perception is too great to be expressed in any construct of language. Perception, the poet's vision of truth, may be communicated in part through "thought" (Browning seems to use "thought" synonymously with "language"), but it can never be fully disclosed, because language, especially at the extremity to which Sordello—and Browning—would like to take it, becomes ineffectual:

> Piece after piece that armour broke away
> Because perceptions whole, like that he sought
> To clothe, reject so pure a work of thought
> As language: Thought may take Perception's place
> But hardly co-exist in any case,
> Being its mere presentment—of the Whole
> By Parts, the Simultaneous and the Sole
> By the Successive and the Many.
>
> (II.601–608)

### BROWNING'S DEDICATION TO HUMANITY

On April 13, 1838, Browning wrote John Robertson that he had decided to leave for Venice, "intending to finish my poem [*Sordello*] among the scenes it describes." [17] Although *Sordello* was not completed

---

[17] Mrs. Sutherland Orr, *Life and Letters of Robert Browning* (Boston, 1891), I, 135.

in Venice, an important event took place during Browning's two-week visit to the city which was to have a great influence on his mature poetry. The description and the meaning of that event are fully recorded by the poet in the last half of *Sordello*'s third book.

Browning depicts himself sitting on the steps of a palace ruin beside a waterway in Venice, musing on his poem, asking himself how he can "exhaust the fit / England gave birth to" (III.681–682). What he thinks he needs is a "queen"—someone who will give him the inspiration to complete the poem. Certainly the beneficial influence will not come from Sordello's character, "no Sordello's Will / Alack!" (III.683–684). With this realization, he turns to find his "queen" among the peasant girls, attractive representatives of youth, vitality, and beauty, who are busy with their daily tasks around him. His difficulty then becomes choosing one among the many to fill his need. Should he single out the girl from Bassano working among the fish boats, one of the girls from Asolo binding lilies for chapel, the girl with the brownest cheeks stooping beneath the arch, or the attractive native of Padua splashing with bare legs in the water?

Suddenly he feels a tug at his coat sleeve, and turns to gaze on a poor, miserable ghost standing at his side:

> You sad disheveled ghost
> That pluck at me and point, are you advised
> I breathe?
>
> (III.700–702)

Prompted by this vision of unhappiness and wretchedness, Browning concedes that despite the efforts of man to convince himself otherwise, happiness is not as widespread over the world as one would like to imagine. To accept these peasant girls as representative of humanity instead of the ghost who has demanded his attention would be false:

> Confess
> You have so niggard stock of happiness
> To share that, do one's uttermost, dear wretch,
> One labours ineffectually stretch
> It o'er you so that mother, children, both
> May equitably flaunt the sumpter-cloth!
>
> (III.709–714)

Browning protests that the original aim of his poetry was not to discuss the limits of happiness and the difficulty of allotting everyone his proper share. Up to now, his purpose has been to express one thought: most of us, peasants or queens, are happy, although we all use different means to gain that happiness. The poet explains that his desire has been to parade these people for the benefit of all humanity. He would admit that there are a luckless few who do not share this state, but their failure to do so comes about not because they were cut off from the world's joy, but because they did not bother to claim their portion:

> be they Peasants, be they Queens,
> Take them, I say, made happy any means,
> Parade them for the common credit, vouch
> A luckless residue we send to crouch
> In corners out of sight was just as framed
> For happiness, its portion might have claimed.
>
> (III.729–734)

Now that this representative of sadness has attracted his attention, all former plans, which could refer to Browning's pre-*Pauline* utopian ambitions, are disturbed: "such my project, baulked / Already" (III.736–737).

At this point Browning declares that he will become the suitor of this symbol of suffering humanity. His pity has been aroused, and he describes her truthfully, avowing that his frankness to her is a sign of his friendship:

> You, no doubt,
> Have the true knack of tiring suitors out
> With those thin lips on tremble, lashless eyes
> Inveterately tear-shot—there, be wise
> Mistress of mine, there, there, as if I meant
> You insult! Shall your friend (not slave) be shent
> For speaking home?
>
> (III.739–745)

The poet is even willing to admit, now that his sympathies have been engaged, that he has always had a weakness for the unlovely and the troubled members of the race, and that this old hag is more attractive, in her own way, than was the idealized conception of humanity he had harbored as a youth:[18]

---

[18] Cf. *Pauline*, l. 425: "Men were to be as gods, and earth as heaven."

                              care-bit erased
          Broken-up beauties ever took my taste
          Supremely, and I love you more, far more
          That [*sic*] she I looked should foot Life's temple-floor.
                                            (III.745–748)

Regret plays no part in Browning's feelings as he contemplates this
change which has taken place in his outlook on life. The ghost and
what she represents are accepted by him and, in a significant passage,
he explains that for a poet to fulfill this role does demand sacrifice, but
that God expects the poets of the world to exert some moral influence
on the rest of humanity and, furthermore, God Himself selects the
burden each one must bear:

                                                    strange
          Such sad chance should produce in thee such change,
          My love! warped men, souls, bodies! yet God spoke
          Of right-hand foot and eye—selects our yoke
          Sordello!
                                            (III.777–781)

Browning is not content merely to state that he will undertake to
champion suffering humanity in his poetry; he goes on to explain
what it is in these warped souls and bodies that specifically interests
him—the problem of evil—and he distinguishes sharply between
poets who take the position that some men are so evil they are beyond
hope, others who choose to ignore the problem altogether, and those,
like himself, who attempt to probe the minds and the motivations of
evil men in order to find some good in them.

There is little sense, Browning believes, in asserting that certain
men are so evil they cannot be saved. Every human being tries to find
a means of staying alive despite his moral condition, and life signifies
potentiality for reform:

                      ask moreover, when they prate
          Of evil men past hope, don't each contrive
          Despite the evil you abuse to live?
                                            (III.784–786)

Even the most spiritually deformed individual attempts, through a
maze of lies, to be loyal to his own conception of truth; and it is
probable that his devious methods and his mode of life are means to

acquire truth, or at least what he envisages as truth, for him. The error lies not so much with the person who refuses to conform to moral law as with the society which, recognizing evil tendencies in certain individuals, denies them common pleasures, and thus forces them to use deceit and treachery to obtain out of life whatever good they can:

> Keeping, each losel, thro' a maze of lies,
> His own conceit of truth? to which he hies
> By obscure tortuous windings, if you will,
> But to himself not inaccessible;
> He sees it, and his lies are for the crowd
> Who cannot see; some fancied right allowed
> His vilest wrong, empowered the fellow clutch
> One pleasure from the multitude of such
> Denied him.
>
> (III.787–795)

Browning is not here rationalizing and justifying evil. He is, however, asserting that evil does exist, and that the common means of rectifying the problem—by punishing or ignoring it—are totally inadequate. We cannot reject our share in the suffering and evil of mankind, and we should avoid increasing our ignorance by proclaiming that everything is as it should be. Some poets contend that hope will be easy to give out, especially after the source of evil has been discovered—if and when this could ever really be accomplished. Until then, they say, listen to my meaningless song which treats of other, more pleasant matters. For such poets, who indulge in triteness when mankind is racked with pain and suffers intense agony, Browning has nothing but contempt:

> if one can't eschew
> One's portion in the common lot, at least
> One can avoid an ignorance increased
> Tenfold by dealing out hint after hint
> How nought is like dispensing without stint
> The water of life—so easy to dispense
> Beside, when one has probed the centre whence
> Commotion's born—could tell you of it all
> —Meantime, just meditate my madrigal
> O' the mugwort that conceals a dewdrop safe!
> What, dullard? we and you in smothery chafe

Babes, baldheads, stumbled thus far into Zin
The Horrid, getting neither out nor in,
A hungry sun above us, sands among
Our throats, each dromedary lolls a tongue,
Each camel churns a sick and frothy chap,
And you, 'twixt tales of Potiphar's mishap
And sonnets on the earliest ass that spoke,
Remark you wonder any one needs choak
With founts about! Potsherd him, Gibeonites.

(III.804–823)

This is neither the utterance of a facile optimist [19] nor the pronounce-ment of a poet who identifies himself with the fastidious Sordello, as Browning once did with the hero of *Pauline* and Paracelsus.

[19] Perhaps because of the reviews his poetry had received, Browning is particu-larly vehement in these lines, and elsewhere in *Sordello*, concerning the relative merits of pretty but meaningless poetry as opposed to philosophic poetry. Although the Browning Societies and their modern followers (e.g., Dallas Kenmare in *Ever a Fighter* [London: John Barrie, 1952], and *An End to Darkness* [London: P. Owen, 1962]), have carried this aspect of Browning to a ridiculous extreme, they are in principle partly justified by Browning himself, especially by his case for philosophic poetry in *Sordello*. It seems as if Naddo, the critic and lackey of whatever poet is in public favor in *Sordello*, serves primarily as a whipping post on which Browning can vent his feelings for those reviewers who had regarded *Pauline* as "a dreamy volume" and had written of *Paracelsus* that "writers will do well to remember . . . that though it is not difficult to imitate the mysticism and vagueness of Shelley, we love him and have taken him to our hearts as a poet, not *because* of these character-istics—but in *spite* of them" (*Athenaeum*, Review of *Paracelsus*, August 2, 1835, p. 640). Naddo is characterized as a "genius-haunter" (II.839) whose theory of literature is adequately summed up in his advice to Sordello:

you're a bard, a bard past doubt,
And no philosopher; why introduce
Crotchets like these? fine, surely, but no use
In poetry—which still must be, to strike,
Based upon common sense; there's nothing like
Appealing to our nature!

. . . . . . . . .
Would you have your songs endure?
Build on the human heart!—Why to be sure
Yours is one sort of heart—but I mean theirs,
Ours, every one's, the healthy heart one cares
To build on!

(II.805–818)

Browning's defense of poetry with moral and philosophic implications is presented negatively in the abuse of Naddo's position (II.838–846, III.247–249), and positively in II.790–804 and III.804–825.

Although the actual circumstance of this vision is clearly not to be taken literally, it is significant that whatever did happen to Browning at Venice seemed important enough for him to break off the logical progress of the poem for the purpose of explaining his change of attitude. DeVane suggests that this conversion signals the end of Browning's interest in romance, as it is exemplified by the second version of *Sordello*, which centered upon the romantic love element between Palma and Sordello. DeVane also notes that although this shift of interest is described as sudden, the suffering Browning saw in Venice only substantiated and brought to the forefront of his mind tendencies previously aroused "by Shelley's liberalism, and more especially by Browning's studies for the *Life of Strafford* in that 'grand epoch' of English history of which he had written in his play." [20] Whatever the preparation and the immediate causes, these "warped men, souls, bodies" and "evil men" supposedly "without hope" become increasingly important as subjects for Browning's poetry after 1840.

With the exception of five short poems published anonymously in the *Monthly Repository*,[21] and *Strafford*, which was the result of his association with Forster and the prose *Life of Strafford*, which he helped Forster finish, *Pauline*, *Paracelsus*, and *Sordello* represent the total of Browning's poetic output published between 1833 and 1840. There is little sense in either belaboring or apologizing for the fact that Browning wrote so much inferior poetry in this period. Indeed, the nature and quantity of theoretical probing in his early work strongly suggests that Browning was not primarily concerned with perfecting the medium of poetry until he knew what he thought he wanted to use that medium for. During these years the interest which drove Browning to write and publish was a theoretical one; technique was subordinated to idea. Even in *Sordello*, the style, or the "brother's speech," was used to illustrate as well as express a theory of poetry.

But despite its difficulty, *Sordello* is for several reasons the most valuable of Browning's early poems. It is simultaneously a review of

---

[20] *Handbook*, p. 81.
[21] Sonnet: "Eyes calm beside thee," *Monthly Repository*, N.S. VIII (October 1834), 712; The King: "A King lived long ago," *Monthly Repository*, N.S. IX (November 1835), 707–708; "Johannes Agricola," *Monthly Repository*, X (January 1836), 45–46; "Porphyria," *Monthly Repository*, X (January 1836), 43–44; Lines: "Still ailing, wind? Wilt be appeased or no?" *Monthly Repository*, N.S. X (May 1836), 270–271.

Browning's career in the 1830's and a preview of what is to follow in the 1840's and 1850's—the conclusion of one phase and the preface to another. Through the depiction of Sordello's shadowy and fruitless life, Browning can be observed, working through the objectivity of the narrative mode, applying and testing out the lessons he had learned in *Pauline* and *Paracelsus* concerning the problems of the disparity between time and eternity, the real and the ideal, the fleshly and the spiritual. Through an examination of the speculations voiced by Browning throughout the poem we are given for the first time an insight into his personal ideas on the poet, on poetry, and on the relationship of each to humanity. *Sordello* is the most objective of Browning's three major early works, but paradoxically, it is also the most revealing one. Browning has learned that poetry cannot express the whole, any more than poets can grasp it, that life itself is "broken and care-bit," and that the poet must accept both the instrument he uses—poetry—and the object he is to work upon—humanity—with their limitations, and attempt to make them better, but not perfect. By bringing his ideas on the poet, poetry, and humanity into cohesion, Browning illustrates that he has effectively solved the moral and aesthetic problems of *Pauline*, and he posits a moral-aesthetic synthesis which is to remain the basic principle of his system of thought throughout the rest of his career. He clearly understands that a disparity exists between what is and what should be, but he also sees that the business of the poet is to bridge that gap and, insofar as he is able, reconcile these apparent opposites. The *Bells and Pomegranates* series, published between 1841 and 1846, represents his first major experiment in searching out the means through which he could realize his plan to build "new structure from the ancient."

## CHAPTER FOUR

# *Bells and Pomegranates*: Technical Experiment— Theoretical Uncertainty

"I shall go to the end of this year, as I now go on—shall print the Eastern play you may remember hearing about—finish a wise meta-physical play (about a great mind and soul turning to ill), and print a few songs and small poems which Moxon advised me to do for popularity's sake! These things done (and my play out), I shall have tried an experiment to the end, and be pretty well contented either way."[1] By the time Browning wrote this to Alfred Domett—May 22, 1842—he had written or had thought seriously about all of the major dramatic pieces published between 1841 and 1846 under the collective title *Bells and Pomegranates* except *Colombe's Birthday* and *Luria*, and had, as the letter shows, recognized that his writing for the stage, which actually began in 1836, was part of "an experiment."[2] The implication that it was to be concluded—"to the end"—and of the phrase "and be pretty well contented either way" would seem to be that Browning was not completely satisfied with the results of his experiment up to this point; and the necessity of accepting Moxon's advice that he publish "a few songs and small poems . . . for popularity's sake" certainly suggests one reason why Browning's experience in writing for the theater was not a very happy one.

This passage points to only a few of the complexities involved in the composition and intended purpose of Browning's *Bells and Pomegranates*, but it does offer one key word—"experiment"—

[1] *Robert Browning and Alfred Domett*, ed. F. G. Kenyon (London: Smith, Elder, 1906), p. 36. The works Browning mentions are *The Return of the Druses*, *A Soul's Tragedy* and *Dramatic Lyrics*.

[2] For probable dates of composition, and dates of publication, see W. C. DeVane, *A Browning Handbook* (2d ed.; New York: Appleton-Century-Crofts, 1955), pp. 91, 98, 104, 132–133, 137, 147, 150, 186, 190.

which is perhaps the only valid generalization one can use in discussing this series of works. In the seven dramas[3] and two volumes of short poems published in this collection, Browning turns away from the theoretical ramblings of *Pauline, Paracelsus,* and *Sordello,* and develops a technique and a poetic form[4] which eventually will enable him to bring to practical realization the moral and aesthetic goals he had set forth in *Paracelsus* and *Sordello.* Rather than advancing in theory,[5] Browning is, as H. B. Charlton explains, "seeking an instrument which at one and the same time will clarify his own sense of things and will transmit that sense to the rest of men with a minimum of distortion. That, after all, is the eternal problem of every poet. A poet must find his idiom . . . ."[6]

Browning's effort to "find his idiom" has received abundant and perceptive critical attention. H. B. Charlton and Park Honan[7] have investigated various aspects of Browning's poetry during this period; and with the help of their insights, one can trace in these works the gradual emergence of poetic skills which, at their highest level of perfection, result in the dramatic monologue. Charlton, who is chiefly concerned with the shorter poems of the period and with the evolution of the dramatic monologue form, explains that in *Dramatic Lyrics* and *Dramatic Romances and Lyrics* Browning is "exploring the range of the dramatic lyric, and feeling for its specific function or its most efficient form."[8] Park Honan, on the other hand, focuses his attention on the dramatic pieces in *Bells and Pomegranates.* Working from *Strafford,* published separately in 1837, through to *A Soul's Tragedy,*

---

[3] Four were written expressly for the stage, as was *Strafford. Pippa Passes, Luria,* and *A Soul's Tragedy* are closet dramas.

[4] The terms "form" and "technique" are used here and throughout this chapter to differentiate between the dramatic poem which centers on a single character who is the speaker, and the means—imagery, diction, rhythm, syntax—employed within that poem to reveal the speaker's character.

[5] An examination of the dramatic pieces in *Bells and Pomegranates* reveals a surprising absence of theoretical probing on Browning's part. Consequently, the emphasis of this chapter is placed on Browning's dissatisfied reaction to his dramatic work, rather than on a detailed treatment of the dramas themselves.

[6] "The Making of the Dramatic Lyric," *Bulletin of John Rylands Library,* XXXV (1952–1953), 354.

[7] Charlton, "The Making of the Dramatic Lyric," pp. 349–384; Park Honan, *Browning's Characters: A Study in Poetic Technique* (New Haven: Yale University Press, 1961), pp. 41–103.

[8] "The Making of the Dramatic Lyric," p. 371.

Honan shows that Browning, through his experiments with syntax, imagery, diction, and rhythm, gradually developed the techniques of characterization fully evident in the later monologues and, in the process of this development, confirmed his growing sense that his true talent lay solely in character delineation. According to Honan, the climax of this period of growth can be seen in "The Tomb at St. Praxed's,"[9] a character-revealing blank verse dramatic monologue published in 1845.

There can be no doubt that Park Honan is correct in his appraisal of the development of Browning's technique: with "The Tomb at St. Praxed's" he had hit upon the synthesis of technique and form that he was later to exploit so fully in *Men and Women*. But a question does arise when we stop to consider whether or not Browning himself understood in 1845 exactly either what he had found or how he was to use it in *Men and Women*. Because he is concerned solely with technique, Honan gives the impression that when Browning wrote his first full-fledged blank verse dramatic monologue in 1845 he became totally dedicated to the monologue in form and technique ("the tragedy [*Luria*] is... interesting for its evidence of Browning's dedication to the monologue form"),[10] and that from this time on, his progress to *Men and Women* was unimpeded. Indeed, Browning did publish a blank verse dramatic monologue in 1845, but this fact only serves to render the apparent lull in his production of dramatic monologues between 1846 and 1852 even more puzzling and problematical.[11] This period of relative inactivity can perhaps be traced to

[9] In the 1849 edition of *Poems* called "The Bishop Orders His Tomb at St. Praxed's." See also Browning's *Essay on Chatterton* (Cambridge, Mass.: Harvard University Press, 1948; first published in the *Foreign Quarterly Review* for July, 1842), and particularly the important introductory chapters by Donald Smalley, who demonstrates that the *Essay* is "a tentative exercise, a laboratory model in the process of special-pleading" (p. 100), and thus that it is another example of Browning's growing interest in character study during the early 1840's.

[10] *Browning's Characters*, p. 103. Honan means that in *Luria*, Browning focuses on a single character, ignores action, and minimizes the role of secondary characters. He also implies that the reason Browning did not employ character-revealing techniques in *Luria* to any great extent was that he had already reached the literal climax of his technical development with "The Tomb at St. Praxed's," published before *Luria* was written.

[11] According to DeVane's conjecture, most of the poems published in *Men and Women* were written between 1852 and 1855. The only poem in *Men and Women*, exclusive of the first nine stanzas of "Saul," which can be dated with any certainty before 1852 is "The Guardian Angel," written in 1848 (*Handbook*, pp. 207, 261–262). DeVane's conjecture seems to be well founded. See Browning's letter to

several causes—Browning's marriage to Elizabeth Barrett in 1846, his desire to rework *Paracelsus* and *Bells and Pomegranates* for the new edition of 1849, or even his grief over the death of his mother in 1849. But more to the point than any of these factors is the basic reason that although Browning had worked out his idiom and form by 1846, he was still unsure about his own role as a poet—still unsure what he wanted to do and could do with the technical instruments he had perfected. This uncertainty, which points to the persistence of the problems that had preoccupied him throughout *Pauline, Paracelsus,* and *Sordello,* is shown in three ways: his curious regression in *Pippa Passes* to a pre-Sordello and even pre-Paracelsus poet-figure who seems to think that life and reality are as simple as the hero of *Pauline* early in his career wished they could be; the dissatisfaction, disappointment, and irresolution expressed in his correspondence with Alfred Domett and Elizabeth Barrett during and after the publication of *Bells and Pomegranates;* and, finally, the difficulty which faced the poet in the composition of "Saul" in 1845.

In *Sordello,* Browning created a poet-figure who dies, after failing both as a poet and as an apostle of social reform, simply because he cannot cope with reality. Browning's own attitude, as expressed in the

John Forster, June 5, 1854: "This is what I have written—only a number of poems of all sorts and sizes and styles and subjects—not written before last year, but the beginning of an expressing the spirit of all the fruits of the years since I last turned the winch of the wine press" (*New Letters of Robert Browning,* ed. W. C. DeVane and Kenneth L. Knickerbocker [New Haven: Yale University Press, 1950], p. 77). Although the literal truth of the statement that none of these poems later to appear in *Men and Women* were written before 1853 is doubtful (see Mrs. 'Sutherland Orr, *Life and Letters of Robert Browning* [Boston, 1891], II, 555; and W. H. Griffin and H. C. Minchin, *The Life of Robert Browning* [New York: Macmillan, 1910], p. 189, who express the generally accepted view that *Childe Roland, Women and Roses,* and *Love Among the Ruins* were written early in 1852), all the evidence available indicates that nothing except "The Guardian Angel" was written before 1852. And the correspondence written after 1852, when Browning began composing *Men and Women,* suggests that his return to serious composition was an especially noteworthy event. On February 24, 1853, Browning wrote to Milsand, "I am writing—a first step towards popularity for me—lyrics with more music and painting than before, so as to get people to hear and see . . . . Something to follow, if I can compass it" (quoted by Griffin and Minchin, *The Life of Robert Browning,* p. 189). Elizabeth Barrett Browning also mentions in 1853 that her husband is writing again: "Robert is working at a volume of lyrics, of which I have seen but a few, and those seemed to me as fine as anything he has done" (EBB to Mr. Chorley, August 10, 1853, *Letters of Elizabeth Barrett Browning,* ed. F. G. Kenyon [London, 1897], II, 131).

various theoretical intrusions noted in the preceding chapter, is that the true poet must fully understand his own limitations, the limitations of his poetry, and the limited possibilities for perfection in the real world. But in *Pippa Passes*, published one year after *Sordello*, Browning depicts a poet-figure who is in, but not of, reality; one who can shape events in the real world with a simple lyric outburst, but who is quite unconscious of her amazing power. Pippa as poet strongly suggests that Browning himself was not prepared in 1841 to apply to his own poetry the theoretical maxims developed during the first decade of his career. *Pippa Passes* represents, I think, a retreat from poetic responsibility. To understand the nature of Browning's regression in *Pippa Passes*, the poem must be considered more thoroughly in its relationship to *Sordello*.

The numerous connections between *Pippa Passes* and *Sordello* indicate that *Pippa* was written immediately after *Sordello* was completed on May 1, 1839, and that it was a direct by-product of the longer poem.[12] Browning's travels in northern Italy in June, 1838, had taken him to Asolo, and the poet's observation of life there contributes to the materials which make up *Pippa Passes*. The topography of Asolo, the conditions in the silk mills, church and political affairs, as well as such character types as mill owners, workers, peasants, police, and itinerant students all appear in the poem.

An even more significant link between the two works is to be found in the relationship between Sordello and Pippa. They are alike in that they are both solitary individuals, both stolen children who are the offspring of wealthy parents, and both poets. But here their similarity ends. The difference between these two figures as poets can be seen in Pippa's connection to the simple barefoot boy who, at the conclusion of *Sordello*, climbs the hillside of Asolo in the early morning and sings

> all the while
> Some unintelligible words to beat
> The lark, God's poet, swooning at his feet.
>
> (VI.866–868)

These "unintelligible words" are Sordello's contribution to the

[12] DeVane, *Handbook*, p. 91. The links I discuss between the two poems are outlined in DeVane's *Handbook*, pp. 91–93, and in Griffin and Minchin's *Life*, pp. 125–126.

human race—"All that's left / Of the Goito lay" (VI.871–872). Pippa, walking on the same hill on a New Year's morning, *is* God's poet, and she sings a song that is not only intelligible but also extremely effective:

> The year's at the spring,
> And day's at the morn:
> Morning's at seven;
> The hill-side's dew-pearled;
> The lark's on the wing,
> The snail's on the thorn;
> God's in his heaven—
> All's right with the world!          (I.253–260) [13]

Sordello is involved, however inadequately, with the problems of reality, and he is concerned with the realization of self through poetic and social action. But he is ineffective in all fields of endeavor: he fails miserably in his love relationship with Palma, in his political aspirations with the Guelphs and Ghibellines, in his attempt to perfect the citizens of Rome, and in his poetic ambitions. Pippa, in contrast, is completely innocent of true involvement with the world of care-bit humanity. Paradoxically, in her purity and aloofness she interferes most effectively with the love affair of Ottima and Sebald, with Italian politics in the Luigi episode, and with the growth to moral responsibility of Jules and the Monsignor. And all of this is achieved through a series of spontaneous unsophisticated and childlike songs.

DeVane states that the contrast between Pippa's effectiveness and Sordello's complete failure to produce tangible results in his dealings with mankind indicates that *Pippa* was "written in a mood of revulsion from the longer poem." [14] And, in my opinion, this reaction to Sordello the poet, and the creation of Pippa and the concept she embodies, is indicative of Browning's own uncertainty about the direction his poetry was to take after 1841.

Pippa may be considered a by-product of Browning's attitude not only toward Sordello, but also toward the inadequate, ineffective, and self-conscious poets of *Pauline* and *Paracelsus*. As the God-centered and unself-conscious agent of the Deity, whose innocent and spontaneous lyric outbursts significantly change the lives of those who hear

---

[13] *Bells and Pomegranates. No. I.—Pippa Passes* (London, 1841).
[14] *Handbook*, p. 93.

her, Pippa represents the creation of an ideal poet-figure.[15] She is, in Browning's own hierarchy of poet types outlined in *Sordello*, neither a false poet who purposely ignores the world's problems and sings of "dew-drops" on "mugworts," nor a true poet who consciously turns to humanity and, forgetful of self, deals with moral problems realistically in a manner which allows man to see himself with an insight otherwise denied him. She is, rather, a regression to the uncomplicated vision of youth, the chastened and purified romantic version of a poet who can do all things for all men and yet never become really involved with them. After the frustrations of *Pauline*, *Paracelsus*, and particularly *Sordello*, it is not altogether surprising that, as a reaction, Browning created a Pippa.[16] But it is surprising that the lack of resolution on Browning's part suggested by *Pippa Passes* continues, as is shown in Browning's correspondence with Alfred Domett and Elizabeth Barrett, throughout this period—and does not cease even after he has found his idiom in 1845.

The letter to Domett quoted at the beginning of this chapter shows that Browning was not happy with his "experiment" in 1842. And although he expresses his discontent even more strongly in that same letter—"At present, I don't know if I stand on head or heels: what men require, I don't know—and of what they are in possession know nearly as little"—he is able to temper his dissatisfaction with a note of encouragement for the future: "The true best of me is to come, and you shall have it . . . ."[17]

[15] E. D. H. Johnson, in *The Alien Vision of Victorian Poetry* (Princeton: Princeton University Press, 1952), perceives a relationship between Pippa, Aprile, and Eglamor. While he would not agree that her presence in the poem constitutes a conceptual inadequacy on Browning's part, he does see her as a type of lyric poet: "She is a child of nature, unlettered, inexperienced, guileless, endowed only with a happy disposition, innocence, and the wisdom of her intuitions" (p. 87).

[16] Although they do not trace the origins of Pippa back to *Sordello*, and although their concern is not primarily with the relationship of Pippa as poet to Browning's career, the following critics have noted the essential weakness of the concept she represents: Arthur E. Dubois, "Robert Browning, Dramatist," *Studies in Philology*, XXXIII (1936), 626–655; Honan, *Browning's Characters*, p. 91; D. C. Wilkinson, "The Need for Disbelief: A Comment on *Pippa Passes*," *University of Toronto Quarterly*, XXIX (1959–1960), 139–151. For opposing points of view, which attribute shrewdness and selfishness rather than naivity to Pippa, see Margaret Eleanor Glen, "The Meaning and Structure of *Pippa Passes*," *University of Toronto Quarterly*, XXIV (1954–1955), 410–426, and Dale Kramer, "Character and Theme in *Pippa Passes*," *Victorian Poetry*, II (Autumn 1964), 241–249.

[17] *Robert Browning and Alfred Domett*, pp. 35–37.

This duality of outlook, the anticipation concerning future works which implies a dissatisfaction with what has already been written, runs throughout the Browning-Domett correspondence. *Dramatic Lyrics* was published on November 26, 1842. The following month Browning wrote Domett: "With this you get some more verses of mine—I shall have more ready ere long, I hope—and better."[18] On March 5, 1843, two months after the publication of *The Return of the Druses*, and one month after that of *A Blot in the 'Scutcheon*, he wrote: "I send the 'Druses' ... and my new play; expect more and better things—I get heart, if not strength, I think."[19] *Colombe's Birthday*, Number Six of *Bells and Pomegranates*, was published in April, 1844. With almost clocklike precision, Browning wrote a letter to Domett a few months later enclosing *Colombe* and half apologizing for it by promising greater things to follow: "I don't think I sent you a copy of my last play—'Colombe': here you shall have it—but I feel myself so much stronger, if flattery not deceive, that I shall stop some things that were meant to follow, and begin again. I really seem to have something fresh to say."[20]

If Browning had actually understood and accepted the significance of his discovery in 1845 when he created the dramatic monologue, it would be logical to expect that his dissatisfaction, his anticipation of leaving behind what he had done and turning to something "fresh" and "better," would disappear, or at least lessen in intensity. Instead, in letters to Domett and Elizabeth Barrett written just at the time when the final piece of *Bells* was being prepared for the publishers (*Luria* and *A Soul's Tragedy*, published April 13, 1846), Browning seems more discontent than he ever had before:

> I have lost, of late, interest in dramatic writing, as you know, and, perhaps, occasion. And, dearest, I mean to take your advice and be quiet awhile and let my mind get used to its new medium of sight; seeing all things, as it does, through you: and then, let all I have done be the prelude and the real work begin.[21]

This morning I went to Moxon's to see about the issue of my number 8,

---

[18] December 13, 1842, *ibid.*, p. 48.
[19] *Ibid.*, p. 51.
[20] July 31, 1844, *ibid.*, p. 106.
[21] February 13, 1846, *The Letters of Robert Browning and Elizabeth Barrett Barrett, 1845–1846* (London, 1899), I, 471.

and last of this series at least. They (*two* plays, to get done) will appear in a fortnight or so, and then I shall breathe for a month or two, God willing, and consider my ways.[22]

All my work (work!)—well, such as it is, it is done—and I scarcely care *how*—I shall be prouder to begin one day—(may it be soon!—) with your hand in mine from the beginning—*that* is a very different thing in its effect from the same hand touching mine *after* I had begun, with no suspicion such a chance could befall! I repeat, both these things, "Luria" and the other, are *manqué*, failures—the life-incidents ought to have been acted over again, experienced afresh; and I had no inclination nor ability. But one day, my siren![23]

One could contend, of course, that these letters are not truly representative of Browning's attitude toward the whole body of *Bells and Pomegranates*, that they are only a result of the numerous difficulties he had with *Luria* and *A Soul's Tragedy*. However, these three passages are consistent in tone with what Browning had written to Domett before the troubles with *Bells* Number Eight arose. In addition, there is the remarkable letter written to Domett on July 13, 1846, when the two final plays had been in print for three months, which sums up everything Browning had written about *Bells and Pomegranates* in his previous correspondence:

As to the obscurity and imperfect expression, the last number of my "Bells," which you get with this, must stand for the best I could do, *four or five months* ago, to rid myself of those defects—and if you judge I have succeeded in any degree, you will not fancy I am likely to relax in my endeavour now. As for the necessity of such endeavour I agree with you altogether: from the beginning, I have been used to take a high ground, and say, all endeavour elsewhere is thrown away. Endeavour *to think* (the real *thought*), to *imagine*, to *create*, or whatever they call it—as well endeavour to add the cubit to your stature! *Nascitur poeta*—and that conceded to happen, the one object of labour is naturally what you recommend to me, and I to myself—nobody knows better, with what indifferent success. But here is, without affectation, the reason why I have gone on so far although succeeding so indifferently: I felt so instinctively from the beginning that unless I tumbled out the dozen more or less of conceptions, I should bear them about forever, and year by year get

[22] March 19, 1846, *Robert Browning and Alfred Domett*, p. 124.
[23] March 25, 1846, *Letters of R.B. and E.B.B.*, II, 2.

straiter and stiffer in those horrible cross-bones with a long name, and at last parturition would be the curse indeed. Mine was the better way, I do calmly believe, for at this moment I feel as everybody does who has worked—"in vain"? no matter, if the work was real. It seems disinspiriting for a man to hack away at trees in a wood, and at the end of his clearing come to rocks or the sea or whatever disappoints him as leading to nothing; but still, turn the man's face, point him to new trees and the true direction, and who will compare his power arising from experience with that of another who has been confirming himself all the time in the belief that chopping wood is incredible labour, and that the first blow he strikes will be sure to jar his arm to the shoulder without shaking a leaf on the lowest bough? I stand at present and wait like such a fellow as the first of these; if the real work should present itself to be done, I shall begin at once and in earnest . . . not having to learn first of all how to keep the axe-head from flying back into my face; and if I stop in the middle, let the bad business of other years show that, I was not idle nor altogether incompetent. . . . I have some important objects in view with respect to my future life—which I will acquaint you with next time I write, when they will be proved attainable or no.[24]

Browning is quite aware that his plays do have "defects" and that because of his work in *Bells and Pomegranates* he has suffered "indifferent success." However, he has learned through practice how to handle the "axe," the instrument of labor, and he is ready to push on "if the real work should present itself." With the acquisition of the poetic skills needed for his craft, Browning has metaphorically reached a clearing in the woods and gained nothing, except, he explains, some experience important with respect to his future life. That is, he has completed *Bells and Pomegranates* and has met Elizabeth Barrett, who does, in fact, turn his face to "new trees and the true direction." But Browning would not reach the final clearing, which we with hindsight can identify as the publication of *Men and Women* in 1855, for nine years. The "real work" of his career would not present itself until 1852. And the question of immediate relevance is why, if he had hit upon the dramatic monologue form as early as 1845, he could not immediately push on to exploit that discovery. Why did Browning spend the years following the publication of the final number of *Bells and Pomegranates* working out, in *Christmas-Eve and Easter-day* and the *Essay on Shelley*, the theoretical possibilities of what that "real work" might be? The

24 *Robert Browning and Alfred Domett*, pp. 126–128.

necessity of this period of self-scrutiny for Browning after 1846 can best be explained by turning to stanzas one through nine of "Saul," a poem which he was unable to complete in 1845, and which would be completed only after he had found his "true direction."[25]

*Pippa Passes* indicates that Browning was aware, as early as 1841, what effect a poet's song should have; and "The Tomb at St. Praxed's" indicates that by 1845 he had discovered the technical means most adequately suited to achieving his poetic aims. "Saul" is another attempt by Browning to find a way in which he could employ his own talent in the task of poetry—to find a way in which he could apply his axe to his tree. And in "Saul" Browning is unwilling to recreate the simple singer and the simple triumph of *Pippa Passes*. From the assured but regressive figure of Pippa, Browning turns to the shepherd singer David for a hesitant, initially unsuccessful, but progressive answer to the problem of searching out the "real work" of his career.

The first nine stanzas of "Saul" were published in *Bells and Pomegranates, No. VII: Dramatic Romances and Lyrics*, in November, 1845.[26] These stanzas, suggested to Browning by his knowledge of Christopher Smart,[27] are based on the story of Saul and David in *I Samuel* 16:14–23. David, the young shepherd minstrel, has been summoned to Saul's tent in the hope that by playing his harp and singing he can relieve the King of the physical and spiritual inertia which envelops him. The poem contains elements of aesthetic and moral interest, which, in their unresolved state in this fragment, reflect the problems Browning encountered in the mid-forties. David is primarily a poet, and the success of his attempt to rejuvenate Saul depends upon his ability to offer the King genuine spiritual insights. But the means by which this task is to be accomplished are not supplied by Smart, nor are they implied by the biblical passage, which states

[25] My position is essentially the same as DeVane's. DeVane states that the two parts of "Saul" serve "as a means of measuring the development of Browning's religious ideas as well as a means of measuring his theory of poetry" (*Handbook*, p. 257). Although the poem is generally accepted as a religious statement, the possibility of considering it for both its moral and aesthetic implications has never been thoroughly investigated. These implications will be examined in the next chapter, in which the completed "Saul" is seen in its relationship to the *Essay on Shelley*.

[26] Pp. 21–22. All citations from "Saul" in this chapter are from the 1845 unfinished version of the poem. The 1845 text is unnumbered.

[27] See W. C. DeVane, *Browning's Parleyings, The Autobiography of a Mind* (New Haven: Yale University Press, 1927), pp. 113–120.

simply that the effect was achieved: "And it came to pass, when the evil spirit from God was upon Saul, that David took an harp, and played with his hand: So Saul was refreshed, and was well, and the evil spirits departed from him" (*I Samuel* 16:23). And in the first nine stanzas of "Saul," Browning himself is not ready to affirm the validity of the resolution—the Incarnation—which is certainly suggested in the image of the crucified Saul which meets David as he enters the tent.

David begins his task by playing on his harp songs with which he thinks the King might be familiar. He plays "the tune all our sheep know" (l. 35), the songs of the quails (l. 41), crickets (l. 42), and jerboa (l. 43), and finally ascends from the level of animal existence to the human, with "the help-tune of our Reapers" (l. 48). After playing music associated with the events around which man's life revolves—death, marriage, and war—David senses a reaction in Saul and stops playing:

> And the tent shook, for mighty Saul shuddered,—
>  And sparkles 'gan dart
> From the jewels that woke in his turban
>  —At once with a start
> All the lordly male-sapphires, and rubies
>  Courageous at heart;
> So the head, but the body still moved not,—
>  Still hung there erect.
>
> (ll. 62–65)

Saul moves his head, thus showing signs of returning physical vitality, but he is still spiritually inert. David then proceeds to celebrate "the wild joys of living" (l. 69), and reaches a climax to his song by affirming that, of all men, Saul has enjoyed the best gifts the world has to offer, and that he, as king, is the epitome of creation:

> Till lo, thou art grown to a monarch,
>  A people is thine!
> Oh all, all the world offers singly,
>  On one head combine,
> On one head the joy and the pride,
>  Even rage like the throe
> That opes the rock, helps its glad labour,
>  And lets the gold go—
> And ambition that sees a sun lead it

> Oh, all of these—all
> Combine to unite in one creature
> —Saul!

(ll. 90–95)

Here the poem ends. The poet David—and Browning—cease poetic activity at the pinnacle of material possibility—at the name and person of King Saul. But material possibility is, as Browning suggests in *Pauline*, insufficient. Throughout his early poetic career Browning consistently strives to achieve a limited degree of participation in that which transcends the purely physical. But because of the knowledge gained through *Paracelsus* and *Sordello*, which had been ignored in *Pippa Passes*, Browning is reticent to move toward the spiritual realm without the assurance that he will not lose the flesh.[28] And yet, as the correspondence cited below implies, he is restless about leaving the celebration of the flesh *in* the flesh.

Browning could not finish "Saul" in 1845 because he himself was uncertain of the applicability of the artistic means necessary to render satisfactorily the religious consolation required to ease Saul's distressed spirit, and of the place of the singer in effecting this cure. That his inability to conclude the poem disturbed him, and that one reason he was unable to do so is related to the inadequacy of his own religious views, is made clear by Elizabeth Barrett in a letter written to Browning on August 27, 1845:

> But your "Saul" is unobjectionable as far as I can see, my dear friend. He was tormented by an evil spirit—but how, we are not told .. and the consolation is not obliged to be definite, .. is it? A singer was sent for as a singer—and all that you are called upon to be true to, are the general characteristics of David the chosen, standing between his sheep and his dawning hereafter, between innocence and holiness .... Where is the wrong in all this? ... How could you doubt about this poem ...[29]

The moral and artistic impasse of which "Saul" is symptomatic is

[28] "Pictor Ignotus," also published in *Dramatic Romances and Lyrics*, 1845, is an interesting example of the consequences of such a movement into the spiritual realm at the expense of the flesh. The "endless cloisters and eternal aisles" which Pictor Ignotus renders with repetitious "cold calm beautiful regard" are artistically inadequate because the painter ignores the "truth made visible in man."

[29] *Letters of R.B. and E.B.B.*, I, 178–179. Irregularities in the ellipses are in the letter itself.

not *the* reason for the barren poetic years following the publication of *Bells and Pomegranates*, but it is at least one reason for the period of inactivity after 1846. *Pauline*, *Paracelsus*, and *Sordello* indicate that for Browning, ideas about poetry are just as important as poetic technique. In *Bells and Pomegranates* the poet can be observed shifting the emphasis from ideas to method, from theory to practice. But despite the technical progress displayed in "The Tomb at St. Praxed's," "Saul" would seem to suggest that by 1845 Browning was yet unclear about exactly how poetry was to achieve the moral ends which he stated in *Sordello* should be its goal. That the answer supplied in *Pippa Passes* was an insufficient one, that it was regressive rather than progressive, was quite possibly realized by Browning when he began the composition of "Saul." For, unlike Pippa, David is thoroughly involved with this one representative of suffering humanity—King Saul. And because Browning is also involved, both with humanity and with the problem of reaching out to humanity through poetry, he cannot acquiesce to the Pippa-like solution offered by Elizabeth Barrett—"and the consolation is not obliged to be definite, . . is it?" By 1845 Browning had found his "idiom," but nevertheless the flow of his poetry was blocked.

Between 1846 and 1850, Browning, with the assistance of Elizabeth Barrett, cleared away the impasse represented by "Saul." The process through which this was accomplished, chronicled in the *Letters of Robert Browning and Elizabeth Barrett Barrett*, *Christmas-Eve and Easter-Day*, and the *Essay on Shelley*, and resulting in the completion of "Saul," will be traced in the following chapter.

CHAPTER FIVE

# Moral-Aesthetic Redefinition:
# 1845–1852

If the two parts of "Saul" are to be considered indicative of the transformation which occurred in Browning's moral-aesthetic theory between 1845 and 1852, it is necessary to investigate briefly the reason for Browning's incapability in 1845 to impart to the poet David the "consolation" or spiritual truth which he must communicate to King Saul. Those who are familiar with the completed "Saul" are aware that the solution to the problem of this consolation as supplied in the second half of the poem centers on David's prophetic vision of the Incarnation, that is, on the figure of Christ as representative of the union of flesh and spirit, of man and God. But the use of Christ in "Saul" would by itself be insufficient proof that Browning's moral-aesthetic took on a new religious perspective after 1845. On the weight of this evidence alone, it could be effectively argued that for this "problem" poem Browning utilized one prominent idea of Christian doctrine, of which he was no doubt aware before 1845, as the easiest way to finish the poem and supply it with a satisfactory and feasible conclusion. However, "Saul" does not stand alone during this period as evidence of Browning's growing interest in the figure of Christ and in specific Christian doctrines associated with Christ. *Christmas-Eve and Easter-Day*, two revisions in the 1849 edition of *Paracelsus*, and the *Essay on Shelley* also point to Browning's increasing conviction that in the figure of the Incarnated Christ he has found both an idea on which to ground his religious faith, and a symbol which at one and the same time states and solves the aesthetic problem of reconciling the fleshly and the spiritual, the spotted and the pure. Again, it should be stressed that the distinction between religious and aesthetic formulations here is an artificial one necessitated for purposes of analysis. Although the chronology of publication (*Paracelsus*, 1849; *Christmas-Eve and Easter-Day*, 1850; *Essay on Shelley*, 1852) seems to indicate that Browning first solidified his religious position and then advanced his aesthetic on the basis of this position, the fact that all of his activities during this period—as worshiper, as poet, as letter writer and critic—were directed toward the fundamental problem of apprehending perfection through imperfection, of somehow fusing apparent opposites, indicates that his religious and aesthetic thoughts developed simultaneously and were mutually dependent.

It would be erroneous to assert that Browning could not complete "Saul" in 1845 because he was unaware of the existence of certain Christian doctrines. One can no doubt assume a knowledge of them on Browning's part as a result of his childhood religious training.[1] However, even though it is undoubtedly true that the Incarnation and its associated doctrines were familiar to Browning before he expressly used them in his poetry after 1846, there is no evidence in his earlier poetry that they constituted an integral part of his thought before 1846. Indeed, Browning's early poetry, though religiously oriented in the sense that it is God-centered, is particularly lacking in a concern with ideas which find their source in the New Testament.[2]

The basic tenet of Browning's thought as a philosopher and as a poet before *Christmas-Eve and Easter-Day* is that man must recognize the limitations of his own powers. For the philosopher, this means that it is impossible to know God directly. For the poet, this means that it is impossible to present an absolute vision of truth in a work of art. The implications of these ideas are examined in *Pauline, Paracelsus*, and *Sordello*. Sordello learns, as did Paracelsus and Aprile, that success as a poet-philosopher depends upon the ability to "fit to the finite his

[1] See, for example, Browning's references to Christ in *Pauline*, ll. 846–854, and *Paracelsus*, V.311. But even in these cases there is no specific interest shown by Browning in the Incarnation or in what it later came to mean to him.

[2] See H. B. Charlton, "Browning As a Poet of Religion," *Bulletin of John Rylands Library*, XXVII (1942–1943), 274. In his *Robert Browning* (New York: Dodd, Mead, 1905), C. H. Herford makes the distinction between "religious" and "Christian" even more explicitly: "In the early Dramatic Lyrics and Romances, and in the plays, there is exquisite rendering of religion, and also of irreligion; but the religion is just the simple faith of Pippa or of Theocrite ["The Boy and the Angel"] that 'God's in his world'; and the irreligion is the Humanist paganism of St. Praxed's, not so much hostile to Christianity as unconscious of it. No single poem written before 1850 shows that acute interest in the problems of Christian faith which constantly emerges in the work of this and the following years" (p. 112).

infinity," or, in other words, to reconcile the soul's aspiration to the inadequate instrument of perception through which it must work. After *Sordello*, however, Browning avoids the issue of exactly how such a compromise is to be achieved in his own poetry. Rather than face this problem in *Pippa Passes*, Browning ignores it by endowing Pippa with a mode of simple lyric expression which exempts her from even recognizing that such a problem exists. But in "Saul," in which the poet David is conceived as a singer who works initially through the realm of temporal experience, Browning is forced to face the critical issue: How much truth can man know, and how is the poet to reconcile the conflicting demands of infinite aspiration and finite ability, a duality of which he is painfully aware even in *Pauline?* Browning, by adopting what appears to be a conscious belief in the man-God synthesis of Christ, by reinforcing the simple theistic belief in God which runs through his early poetry with Christian doctrine, comes to understand the means by which he himself can effectively "fit to the finite his infinity." The practical poetic compromise represented by the dramatic monologues of *Men and Women* (1855), a form which dwells on the flesh, but nevertheless gives intimations of the spirit, which allows the poet to harness his own spiritual powers of imagination and understanding in a concentrated dramatic moment bounded by the limitations of time, space, and language, is analogous to the compromise Browning envisaged as constituting the essence of the Christian doctrine which centers on the Incarnation.[3] God worked through the flesh to reach man; man must work through the flesh to reach God. Through the revisions of the 1849 edition of *Paracelsus*, *Christmas-Eve and Easter-Day*, the *Essay on Shelley*, and the second half of "Saul," the major ideas of which are foreshadowed in the letters of Browning and Elizabeth Barrett in 1845 and 1846, it is possible to trace Browning's search for and discovery of beliefs, sects, images, and people that make the ideal actual, the infinite finite.

Chronologically, the first signpost in Browning's poetry after 1846 that indicates the direction in which his religious thought is turning appears in two revisions in *Paracelsus* printed with *Bells and*

---

[3] This formulation, and indeed my whole approach to Browning, is heavily indebted to the work of W. O. Raymond. See especially " 'The Jewelled Bow': A Study in Browning's Imagery and Humanism," in *The Infinite Moment and Other Essays in Robert Browning* (2d ed.; Toronto: University of Toronto Press, 1965), pp. 193–213.

*Pomegranates* in *Poems* in 1849.[4] In Canto Two of the 1835 version of *Paracelsus*, Aprile offers Paracelsus the key to the failure of his quest for infinite knowledge by explaining that he, too, in his search for infinite love, had rejected the "weeds" of existence. Man's quest for God, Aprile explains, must take cognizance of the limited means at his disposal: the imperfect and the finite is the proper sphere of man. The solution lies not in an absolute vision of truth, but in the awareness that God can best be apprehended through His creations. Aprile dies with this message on his lips: "God is the PERFECT POET, / Who in his person acts his own creations" (ll. 610–611). When, in Canto Five, Paracelsus finally sees the futility of his Promethean aspiration, the words he speaks clearly illustrate that he has accepted the validity of Aprile's injunction in Canto Two. God is not inaccessible to man. Rather,

> He dwells in all,
> From life's minute beginnings, up at last
> To man—the consummation of this scheme
> Of being—the completion of this sphere
> Of life.
>
> (V.692–696)

These two passages accurately sum up Browning's attitude toward God in *Paracelsus*. The poem is certainly God-centered, but there is no recognition of Christ as the God-man synthesis. However, in the 1849 edition of *Paracelsus*, Browning brings the Incarnation into the poem by adding the following lines to Aprile's dying speech:

> God is the PERFECT POET,
> Who in creation acts his own conceptions.
> Shall man refuse to be aught less than God?
> Man's weakness is his glory—for the strength
> Which raises him to heaven and near God's self,
> Came spite of it: God's strength his glory is,

[4] See *Letters of Robert Browning, Collected by Thomas J. Wise*, ed. Thurman L. Hood (New Haven: Yale University Press, 1933), p. 14. Browning apparently started thinking about this collected edition early in 1847. His letter to Moxon, written on February 24, 1847, is his first reference to such an edition: "But the point which decided me to wish to get printed over again was the real good I thought I could do to *Paracelsus, Pippa*, and some others; good, not obtained by cutting them up and reconstructing them, but by affording just the proper revision they ought to have had before they were printed at all."

For thence came with our weakness sympathy
Which brought God down to earth, a man like us.

(ll. 663–670)

In his attempt to prove that Browning's conception of love in Canto Five is "a Christian representation of love," W. O. Raymond refers to these added lines in Canto Two. By doing so, he gives the false impression that the Incarnation was an integral part of Browning's thought in 1835. Concerning Aprile's position he states: "That Browning is here representing Aprile's error as due to a failure to grasp that conception of love which may be regarded as pre-eminently Christian, is made explicit in lines added by the poet, in one edition of *Paracelsus*, at the end of Aprile's dying speech." [5] Raymond quotes the 1849 addition, and then carries its meaning over into Canto Five, which was not significantly altered in the 1849 edition: "The final attainment of Paracelsus, as portrayed in the fifth canto, is an expansion of the idea of love set forth in these lines. It is a description of love which, without direct Christian reference, is permeated by Browning's religious sympathies." [6] Then, in his summary statement describing Browning's conception of love in the poem, he ventures even further on the strength of the 1849 version of Aprile's speech: "Such a portrayal of love is an expression of the spirit of the Christian *Magnificat*, rather than of romantic or Platonic idealism, and it manifestly has its sources in Browning's deep religious convictions, above all his appreciation of the supreme truth revealed through the doctrine of the Incarnation." [7]

My purpose here is not to attempt to refute Raymond, since he is not primarily interested in Browning's development in this particular essay; but it should be pointed out that although the spirit of love in *Paracelsus* may be religious, it is not in the spirit of the Christian *Magnificat*. And it seems as though Browning himself recognized that the amplification of Aprile's speech in Canto Two was inconsistent with the original purpose of the poem, which was to trace the growing awareness of Paracelsus through the vicissitudes of his own experience, not through a sudden revelation of the Incarnation; in the 1863 edition of *Paracelsus*, Aprile's reference to the Incarnation was dropped from the text.

[5] *The Infinite Moment*, p. 171.
[6] *Ibid.*, p. 171.
[7] *Ibid.*, p. 174.

The significance of these lines, then, is that in 1849 Browning appears to have accepted the doctrine of the Incarnation and, by applying it as a solution in *Paracelsus* to the disparity between the finite and the infinite, he was giving to a theory he had held for some time a new perspective—a doctrinal foundation.

There is one more revision in *Paracelsus* for the 1849 edition which, although extremely minor in itself, does reinforce the contention that in 1849 Browning's thought was becoming oriented to religious themes more than it had formerly been. In the 1835 edition of *Paracelsus*, a metaphor occurs in which the figures on a church spire are compared to a group of colorfully clad Jews:

> See how bright St. Saviour's spire
> Flames in the sunset; all its figures quaint
> Gay in the glancing light: you might conceive them
> A troop of yellow-vested, white-hair'd Jews.

(V.333-336)

As it stands, the metaphor is clear enough. But in 1849 Browning added a single line which places the image in a distinctly Christian context, and which also points to the major theme of *Christmas-Eve and Easter-Day*: "Bound for their own land where redemption dawns!" One year after the revised edition of *Paracelsus* was published, *Christmas-Eve and Easter-Day* appeared—a pair of poems devoted to the ways and means of redemption.

Although there is considerable disagreement among Browning's critics as to exactly what these poems signify about the poet's actual religious position in 1850, there is general agreement that they each represent a serious approach on Browning's part to religious problems he had ignored in his poetry up to this time.[8] My purpose in treating

[8] This contentious question has given rise to at least three general points of view, and even within these approaches there are considerable differences of opinion. The most widely held is that Browning, through Elizabeth Barrett, returned to the Evangelical faith of his mother. See A. W. Crawford, "Browning's *Christmas-Eve*," *Methodist Review*, CX (May 1927), 379–382, and "Browning's 'Saul,'" *Queen's Quarterly*, XXXIV (1927), 448–454; DeVane, *A Browning Handbook* (2d ed.; New York: Appleton-Century-Crofts, 1955), pp. 194–205; Betty Miller, *Robert Browning: A Portrait* (New York: Charles Scribner's Sons, 1953), pp. 173–174; William L. Phelps, *Robert Browning* (2d ed.; Indianapolis: Bobbs-Merrill, 1932), pp. 405–410; W. O. Raymond, *The Infinite Moment*, pp. 24–45. At the other extreme are those who hold that Browning belonged to no specific sect. See Kingsbury Badger, "'See the Christ Stand!': Browning's Religion," *Boston*

*Christmas-Eve and Easter-Day* here is not to add another definition of Browning's "religion" to the numerous ones already in existence, but primarily to consider these poems as reflections of the religious ideas Browning was exploring and assimilating during this stage of his development and, further, to illustrate that these ideas embody, in their preoccupation with bringing into a harmonious relationship the human and the divine, the basic problem of poetic theory which Browning was investigating at the same time.

Even if we cannot know the exact significance with regard to Browning's own position of the narrator's final choice of the Evangelical chapel over Roman Catholicism and Higher Criticism in *Christmas-Eve*, we certainly can read these two poems and draw definite conclusions as to what Browning considered the essential doctrines of his personal religious creed. Both poems indicate that Browning was quite willing to consider a number of religious approaches—Evangelicalism, Roman Catholicism, and Biblical Criticism in *Christmas-Eve*, and the cynical, relaxed approach to Christianity and its opposite, the narrowly ascetic approach which stresses the difficulty of belief in *Easter-Day*—and single out from these analyses elements of belief he himself could either accept or reject. The positive results of this liberal Christian survey by Browning may be summarized as follows: belief in the divinity of Christ, in the power of Divine love, and in the realization that through human love man in some way partakes of God's love; a growing awareness of the limitations of the power of reason, which, in *Paracelsus*, was equated with the power of love; and finally, an understanding that the world must be seen not as an end in itself, but as a means to a higher goal.

In *Christmas-Eve* Browning finds something valuable, and also something thoroughly unpleasant, in both the Roman Catholic and the Evangelical celebrations of Christ's birth. He completely rejects the purely intellectual approach of Biblical Criticism. The poem opens with the narrator standing in the doorway of an Evangelical chapel on

---

*University Studies in English*, I (1955), 53–73; Francis R. Duckworth, *Browning: Background and Conflict* (New York: E. P. Dutton, 1932), 188–191. Hoxie N. Fairchild, sole exponent of the third viewpoint, thinks that Browning did return to his mother's religion through Elizabeth Barrett, but that this religion was an extremely liberal form of Evangelicalism, rather than the narrow and bigoted sect depicted in *Christmas-Eve*. See *Religious Trends in English Poetry, 1830–1880* (New York: Columbia University Press, 1957), IV, 49–57, 134–166.

Christmas Eve. Quite by chance, he has taken refuge here from a storm which caught him on the open common that lies in front of the meeting house. It immediately becomes evident that if Browning is in any way attracted by the Evangelical sect, it is not because of his admiration for the congregation of this chapel, nor because of the spiritual edification offered by the preacher. A parody of the biblical parable of the shepherd and his flock is employed to convey the narrator's first impressions of the Zion-bound procession passing by him into the body of the church. The people are sheep, the door is a gate, the entrance way is a cattle chute, and the interior of the structure is a sheepfold:

> Heaven knows how many sorts of hands
> Reached past me, groping for the latch
> Of the inner door that hung on catch,
> More obstinate the more they fumbled,
> Till, giving way at last with a scold
> Of the crazy hinge, in squeezed or tumbled
> One sheep more to the rest in fold,
> And left me irresolute, standing sentry
> In the sheepfold's lath-and-plaster entry,
> Four feet long by two feet wide,
> Partitioned off from the vast inside.
>
> (ll. 8–18)[9]

The sheep are repulsive both in their physical appearance and in their attitude toward this uninvited guest. Except for the "tall yellow man, like the Penitent Thief, / With his jaw bound up in a handkerchief," who fails to notice the narrator because his eyelids are "screwed together tight" as if he is leading himself in "by some inner light" (ll. 81–84), each member of the congregation challenges his right to participate in their service. They, after all, are the chosen ones, and their question, "'What, you, the alien, you have ventured / To take with us, elect, your station?'" (ll. 87–88), so nettles the speaker that he resolves "'despite the pretty perfection'" to which these so-called Christians carry their "'trick of exclusiveness,'" to enter the chapel, call out for "'Shares'" (ll. 109–115), and make known his demands:

[9] Citations from *Christmas-Eve and Easter-Day* are from the unnumbered text in Robert Browning's *Christmas-Eve and Easter-Day* (London, 1850). Line numbers are added.

"shut your mouth, and open your Testament,
And carve me my portion at your quickliest!"

(ll. 121–122)

And he does enter, but the "hot smell and the human noises," and "the preaching-man's immense stupidity" (ll. 140–144) quickly drive him out again. He will return later and, despite the disagreeable elements he has encountered here, he will decide to remain; but first he is given the chance to consider two alternatives.

Standing on the common outside the chapel, the narrator suddenly becomes aware of a double rainbow in the sky, and looking up, he beholds a vision of Christ. Browning does not attempt to describe the Christ figure, but in keeping with the spirit of the occasion on which the incident is supposed to take place—Christmas—and indicative of his own outlook throughout all the work of this period, he stresses Christ's humanity:

All at once I looked up with terror.
He was there.
He Himself with His human air.

(ll. 431–433)

The narrator grasps the hem of Christ's garment and is suddenly carried to Rome and the midnight Mass at St. Peter's Basilica.

A number of interesting points emerge from the narrator's description of his experience in Rome which are suggestive of Browning's attitude toward Catholicism. To begin with, Christ *is* present at this service: "He will go / And sit with these in turn, I know" (ll. 611–612). Further, Browning describes the Consecration so accurately and with such a reverential attitude that it is difficult to believe he did not appreciate at least its symbolic significance. The Mass appeals to Browning because it evokes in him, and in its participants, an awareness of both Christ's divine and human attributes:

Earth breaks up, time drops away,
In flows heaven, with its new day
Of endless life, when He who trod,
Very Man and very God,
This earth in weakness, shame and pain,
Dying the death whose signs remain
Up yonder on the accursed tree,—

> Shall come again, no more to be
> Of captivity the thrall,
> But the one God, all in all,
> King of kings, and Lord of lords,
> As His servant John received the words,
> "I died, and live for evermore!"
>
> (ll. 585–597)

Although he does not like the dogmatic assurance with which Rome asserts its doctrines, Browning is able to see that through its "errors and perversities" (l. 619) there is ample evidence of Christian love:

> I see the error; but above
> The scope of error, see the love.—
> Oh, love of those first Christian days!
> —Fanned so soon into a blaze,
> From the spark preserved by the trampled sect.[10]
>
> (ll. 649–653)

The worshipers in the Basilica are "So many species of one genus, / All with foreheads bearing *Lover*" (ll. 707–708), and in this capacity to love lies their chief merit. Then, after deciding what attracts him to this mode of belief—its cognizance of the possibility of the union of man with God through love—as well as what repels him—its over-indulgence in embellishment, which tends to detract from the intensity of that union—the narrator suddenly finds himself in Göttingen outside the Higher Criticism lecture hall.

The "hawk-nosed, high-cheek-boned Professor" (l. 816), representative of the rationalistic approach to the birth of Christ, has a dual purpose in his lecture. First, he is concerned with explaining just how this myth of Christ has come about:

> How the ineptitude of the time,
> And the penman's prejudice, expanding
> Fact into fable fit for the clime,
> Had, by slow and sure degrees, translated it
> Into this myth, this Individuum.
>
> (ll. 874–878)

[10] For a thorough analysis of Browning's attitude toward Roman Catholicism over the range of his career, see Boyd Litzinger's "Robert Browning and the Babylonian Women," *Baylor Browning Interests*, No. 19 (Waco, 1962).

To his second query, whether or not Christ was real—if he actually did exist at one time in history—the Professor concludes that Christ did indeed exist, but that he was a good man and nothing more:

> A Man!—a right true man, however,
> Whose work was worthy a man's endeavour!
>
> (ll. 881–882)

The narrator does admit, in his mood of easy tolerance, that although love is dead in the lecture hall its "ghost" might yet remain behind. This critic grinds the "Pearl of Price" (l. 1080) to dust with the use of reason, but he does at least advise his listeners that they might just as well "venerate the Myth" (l. 1091) he has experimented with, rather than arbitrarily choose some other man to worship. However, the narrator's tolerant approach does not seem to be representative of Browning's view of the matter. The geniality of the narrator is a device used by the poet to effect the transition out of the lecture hall back to the Evangelical chapel. As he basks in this "lazy glow of benevolence" (l. 1170), the hem of Christ's garment is swept from the speaker's hand. Only after deciding that the loss of the garment means he too must choose one "chief / Best way of worship" (ll. 1173–1174) is the narrator again able to grasp the hem, which then carries him back to his starting point. But before the narrator slips into his genial tolerance concerning the German lecturer, while he is still consciously responding to the commands transmitted to him through the garment he holds, we are given a view that is closer to Browning's own regarding the merits of Higher Criticism. This statement also summarizes Browning's opinion of the Evangelical chapel and the Roman Catholic Basilica:

> I could interpret its command.
> This time He would not bid me enter
> The exhausted air-bell of the Critic.
> Truth's atmosphere may grow mephitic
> When Papist struggles with Dissenter,
> Impregnating its pristine clarity,
> —One, by his daily fare's vulgarity,
> Its gust of broken meat and garlic;
> —One, by his soul's too-much presuming,
> To turn the frankincense's fuming
> And vapours of the candle starlike

> Into the cloud her wings she buoys on:
> And each, that sets the pure air seething,
> Poisoning it for healthy breathing—
> But the Critic leaves no air to poison;
> Pumps out by a ruthless ingenuity
> Atom by atom, and leaves you—vacuity.
>
> (ll. 900–916)

Of the three positions discussed, the vacuum created by the intellectual approach of the Biblical critic is the only one totally rejected.[11]

Having explored these three distinct modes of belief, the narrator again finds himself in the Evangelical chapel. His first visit to Zion proved extremely distasteful, but now the speaker feels an urgency to align himself with one specific religious position. The Roman Catholic ritual is permeated with love, but there are too many incidentals added to the service which detract from its original purpose—to bring the worshiper closer to God. The Higher Critic depends solely on reason. The Evangelicals are vulgar, but the narrator decides that here, where the fewest impediments are placed between the believer and his religious experience, he must cast his lot:

> I, then, in ignorance and weakness,
> Taking God's help, have attained to think
> My heart does best to receive in meekness
> This mode of worship, as most to His mind,
> Where earthly aids being cast behind,
> His All in All appears serene,
> With the thinnest human veil between.
>
> (ll. 1305–1311)

Whether or not Browning himself actually adopted the Evangelical position in practice is of little real consequence in this discussion.[12] What is important is that, typical of all of Browning's choices during

[11] See W. O. Raymond, "Browning and Higher Criticism," in *The Infinite Moment*, pp. 19–51.

[12] Browning's correspondence, which is usually cited in an attempt to give some meaning to the inconclusive evidence in the poem, serves only to confuse the issue further. The letters only add to the impression gained from *Christmas-Eve* that Browning's religion is intensely personal, extremely liberal, and, for all practical purpose, totally undefinable. See *The Letters of Robert Browning and Elizabeth Barrett Barrett* (London, 1899), II, 427–428, August 15, 1846; and II, 434, August 17, 1846.

this period, his narrator picks the most fleshly of the three alternatives as the surest route to God, and that certain ideas emerge from the poem which are attributable to Browning because they are consistent with similar ideas in *Easter-Day*, the *Essay on Shelley*, and later in *Men and Women*: the necessity of belief in Christ as the mediator between the human and the divine, the value of love shared by man and God as the instrument which makes such mediation possible, and the indefiniteness of the assurances for faith provided by reason.

*Easter-Day* is organized around a debate between two Christians who represent diametrically opposed positions to the problem of belief. The narrator's constant complaint is that from his consideration of the various aspects of faith he derives little satisfaction. He finds only "How very hard it is to be / A Christian!" (ll. 1–2), because there is really no certitude possible for one who desires absolute assurance that what he believes is correct. He is also troubled because, contrary to his natural impulses, his conscience warns him that he must not take pleasure in the good things of the material world. In reply, the detached Christian who feels that "'I should not find it hard / To be a Christian'" (ll. 140–141), states that he is quite satisfied to base his belief on probability and uncertainty: "'You must mix some uncertainty / With faith, if you would have faith *be*'" (ll. 71–72). Furthermore, he contends that those who would renounce the world are only showing ingratitude to God for the good things of the world He has provided:

> Such is man's usual gratitude,
> Such thanks to God do we return,
> For not exacting that we spurn
> A single gift of life.
>
> (ll. 205–208) [13]

But the narrator will not be content with this explanation. Do you think, he asks, that Christ lived and died for us "Only to give our joys a zest, / And prove our sorrows for the best?" (ll. 240–241). And is it not written in several places, he continues, that man must reject the world if he is to be saved:

> there be certain words, broad, plain,
> Uttered again and yet again,

[13] The narrator speaks these words, but, as he explains, he is voicing the opinion of his friend.

> Hard to mistake, to overgloss—
> Announcing this world's gain for loss,
> And bidding us reject the same:
> The whole world lieth (they proclaim)
> In wickedness,—come out of it!—
>
> (ll. 258–264)

He concludes this torrent of negativistic pietism with a plea for his friend's advice. The easy believer sees not only that his debating opponent is already convinced that it is hard to be a Christian, but that he is resolved to make the most of his self-inflicted suffering, so he attempts to placate his anxieties by agreeing that:

> "I'd take, by all means, in your place,
> "The safe side, since it so appears:
> "Deny myself, a few brief years,
> "The natural pleasure, leave the fruit
> "Or cut the plant up by the root."
>
> (ll. 269–273)

Then the narrator changes his mind. Evidently he is one of those individuals who are never content with anything they are told, for he now contemplates the possibility that the rejection of pleasure might not, after all, be profitable. How is he to know that he would not be giving up everything for nothing:

> If after all we should mistake,
> And so renounce life for the sake
> Of death and nothing else?
>
> (ll. 297–299)

This is enough to make the easy believer impatient. He lives in "trusting ease" (l. 329), and he warns his friend that he will receive no thanks for trying to make things hard for him too. But the speaker of the poem is not so easy to ward off. He announces that he has a story, an account of a vision he experienced three years before on the common where the chapel is situated which "our friend" talked about "the other day" (l. 380), that will convince his listener "How hard it is to really be / A Christian" (ll. 367–368).

Thus far in the poem it is impossible to detect any specific ideas which can be attributed directly to Browning himself. The debate carried on between the two believers is not depicted in a way which reveals the thoughts of the author on the problems discussed, and what we know of Browning's own ideas through an examination of *Christmas-Eve* discourages any attempt to identify him with either the "trusting ease" of the one Christian, or the initially narrow-minded ascetic viewpoint of the other. However, in the next section of the poem, Browning does enunciate his own ideas through the voice of God, who counsels the troubled narrator about the correct use of earthly aids in the struggle for belief. Since the narrator underwent this experience three years before the recitation in *Easter-Day*, we can deduce that he totally missed the significance of what God told him. Indeed, he continues to insist, at the end of the poem, that life for him is a "warfare." But it is the perversion of his own mind which convinces him that severity, hardship, and difficulty of belief are his personal burdens in life. The ideas expressed in his dream-vision could not have led him to such a conclusion, nor did they lead Browning, whose thought they reflect, to adopt such a severe approach to life.

The vision came to the narrator on the common as he was meditating on just such problems as he has been discussing with his friend. While engaged in his thoughts on the problems of belief and disbelief, the question occurred to him:

> 'How were my case, now, should I fall
> 'Dead here, this minute—do I lie
> 'Faithful or faithless?'
>
> (ll. 401–403)

Suddenly "all the midnight round" became "One fire" (ll. 510–511), and he was shocked to find that Judgment Day had indeed arrived. The question of whether he would be found "Faithful or faithless" on that fatal day is answered immediately—he would be faithless:

> There, stood I, found and fixed, I knew,
> *Choosing the world.* The choice was made—
> And naked and disguiseless stayed,
> And unevadeable, the fact.
>
> (ll. 559–562)

Then the voice of God confirms the narrator's evaluation of his own weakness in the expressed preference for the imperfection of earth to the perfection of heaven:

>                                   "This world,
> "This finite life, thou hast preferred,
> "In disbelief of God's own word,
> "To Heaven and to Infinity.
> "Here, the probation was for thee,
> "To show thy soul the earthly mixed
> "With Heavenly, it must choose betwixt.
> "The earthly joys lay palpable,—
> "A taint, in each, distinct as well;
> "The Heavenly flitted, faint and rare,
> "Above them, but as truly were
> "Taintless, so in their nature, best,
> "Thy choice was earth: thou didst attest
> "'Twas fitter spirit should subserve
> "The flesh, than flesh refine to nerve
> "Beneath the spirit's play.
>
> .   .   .   .   .   .   .   .   .   .   .
>
>                                   "Thou art shut
> "Out of the Heaven of Spirit; glut
> "Thy sense upon the world: 'Tis thine
> "For ever—take it!"                   (ll. 675–707)

This passage may seem, on the surface, particularly if we accept it as a pronouncement by Browning of his own position, to contradict the moral philosophy so clearly outlined in *Paracelsus* (and less clearly in *Sordello*), which celebrates the value of imperfection. When Elizabeth Barrett "complained of the *asceticism*" [14] of the piece, it might well have been this passage, together with the narrator's previously stated fear of enjoying anything created, to which she was referring. But if we consider the circumstances in the poem under which this judgment is passed, its severity is justified. Here Browning is examining the same question treated in *Paracelsus*, but he is looking at it from the opposite end of the telescope. Paracelsus and Aprile tried to bypass the earth to gain Heaven, but because of their temporal limitations they failed. The narrator of *Easter-Day* is lifted out of the temporal circumstance which necessitates an appreciation and acceptance of imperfection, and he is placed in the either/or position which Paracelsus and Aprile longed for but could never attain. Under this condition, Browning is

---

[14] EBB to Mrs. Jameson, May 4, 1850, *Letters of Elizabeth Barrett Browning*, ed. F. G. Kenyon (London, 1897), I, 449.

saying, there is no doubt about the choice which must be made. Things of earth are tainted; things of heaven are taintless. The narrator has decided that he prefers the tainted, and his sentence is suited to that decision. The discussion which ensues between the speaker and God centering on the relative value of earthly attributes does not contradict, but substantiates the opinions concerning imperfection expressed by Browning in *Paracelsus* and *Sordello*, as well as those on love and reason in *Christmas-Eve*. God explains to the narrator how things of earth should be viewed when man *is* immersed in them, and these explanations are much more tolerant of imperfection than those stated in the situation in which the speaker found himself at the moment of judgment. The world should not be utterly rejected, but should be viewed as something which can help man to a higher goal.

Since he has been given permission to glut himself on the world's riches, the narrator declares that he will make full use of his opportunity:

> 'How? Is mine,
> 'The world?' (I cried, while my soul broke
> Out in a transport) 'Hast Thou spoke
> 'Plainly in that? Earth's exquisite
> 'Treasures of wonder and delight,
> 'For me?'
>
> (ll. 708–713)

But God points to the futility of delight in beauty for its own sake. The beauty of earth is good because it presages a greater beauty which will one day be within man's grasp, but it is not sufficient to satisfy for an eternity:

> "All partial beauty was a pledge
> "Of beauty in its plenitude:
> "But since the pledge sufficed thy mood,
> "Retain it—plenitude be theirs
> "Who looked above!"
>
> (ll. 779–783)

Next, the narrator turns to art, which, he presumes, makes the beauty of nature more resplendent by adding man's touch to it:

> 'Henceforth my part
> 'Be less with Nature than with Art!
> 'For Art supplants, gives mainly worth

'To Nature; 'tis Man stamps the earth—
'And I will seek his impress.'

(ll. 787–791)

Again, God corrects this view by telling the narrator what Aprile and Sordello learned in their quests—that art can never apprehend ultimate truth. The highest goal that art can achieve is to body forth parts of the whole, hints of the truth:

"Obtain it," said the Voice.
"The one form with its single act,
"Which sculptors labored to abstract,
"The one face, painters tried to draw,
"With its one look, from throngs they saw!
"And that perfection in their soul,
"These only hinted at? The whole,
"They were but parts of?"

(ll. 795–802)

In desperation the speaker turns to reason. Now, however, he shows signs of understanding his mistake in attaching all value to earthly things, for he not only makes his choice but also anticipates God's answer by explaining himself the futility of relying on reason:

'Still, I can profit by late found
'But precious knowledge. Mind is best—
'I will seize mind, forego the rest
'And try how far my tethered strength
'May crawl in this poor breadth and length.

. . . . . . . . . . .

'Let me alone! No answer, pray,
'To this! I know what Thou wilt say!
'All still is earth's,—to Know, as much
'As Feel its truths, which if we touch
'With sense or apprehend in soul,
'What matter? I have reached the goal—
'"Whereto does Knowledge serve!" will burn
'My eyes, too sure, at every turn!'

(ll. 885–910)

Finally, the narrator's search within the dream-vision comes to an end with the recognition that love, and only love, is the one quality accessible to man upon which he may completely depend for salvation:

"I let the world go, and take love!" (l. 946). In His answer to this decision, God explains why love is such an important aspect of man's existence. Love is the one attribute which envelops all things on earth, and its value is proven by the fact that through His love for man, and as evidence of it, God became flesh and suffered death. God admonishes the narrator that his greatest error has been in forgetting that all things of earth are fitted to man's needs, and that the basis of the plan of salvation is love itself. W. O. Raymond's statement concerning *Paracelsus* is most appropriate when applied to this explanation of the value of love. *Easter-Day* is truly written in the spirit of the Christian *Magnificat*, and its source does have its deepest roots in Browning's religious convictions and in his appreciation of the truth revealed through the Incarnation:

> "Is this thy final choice?
> "Love is the best? 'Tis somewhat late!
> "And all thou dost enumerate
> "Of power and beauty in the world,
> "The mightiness of love was curled
> "Inextricably round about.
> "Love lay within it and without,
> "To clasp thee,—but in vain! Thy soul
> "Still shrunk from Him who made the whole,
> "Still set deliberate aside
> "His love!—Now take love! Well betide
> "Thy tardy conscience! Haste to take
> "The show of love for the name's sake,
> "Remembering every moment Who
> "Beside creating thee unto
> "These ends, and these for thee, was said
> "To undergo death in thy stead
> "In flesh like thine: so ran the tale.
> "What doubt in thee could countervail
> "Belief in it? Upon the ground
> "'That in the story had been found
> "'Too much love? How could God love *so*?
> "He who in all his works below
> "Adapted to the needs of man,
> "Made love the basis of the plan."          (ll. 971–995)

But despite the clarity of this vision, and of the truths communicated through it, the narrator of the poem has not been convinced that salvation is possible without undue asceticism. He misses the point of his lesson: a Christian must use the world wisely and moderately, not scourge himself by denying its pleasures or overvalue it as an end in itself:

> Thank God, no paradise stands barred
> To entry, and I find it hard
> To be a Christian, as I said!
>
> (ll. 1043–1045)

Browning concludes the poem by suggesting, however, that even for this man, as for all believers who have difficulty in properly evaluating the helps they are offered for salvation, there is some hope. That hope rests on the mercy of God as exemplified by the life, death, and resurrection of Christ:

> But Easter-Day breaks! But
> Christ rises! Mercy every way
> Is infinite,—and who can say?
>
> (ll. 1053–1055)

*Christmas-Eve* and *Easter-Day* are quite dissimilar in their approaches to the problem of belief. As W. C. DeVane comments, *Christmas-Eve* examines "man's relation to the various creeds," while *Easter-Day* explores more directly man's "relation to Christ." [15] Nevertheless, each poem dwells on the same basic themes, and through a study of these themes the range and depth of Browning's thought on religious matters in 1850 is revealed. There is no doubt that after 1846 Browning, through the influence of Elizabeth Barrett, made a significant advance in his religious development. In *Christmas-Eve and Easter-Day* Browning moves from the God-centered nondoctrinal Christianity of his early poetry to an equally liberal, but more specifically doctrinal, mode of belief. He adopts an intense conviction in the efficacy of the Incarnation and its related doctrines, and he destroys the equation of love and knowledge established in *Paracelsus* by devaluing reason and emphasizing the power of love. This advance is, however, not primarily important in itself, but is relevant in this study only insofar as it helps illuminate the growth of Browning's aesthetic theory which took place at the same time. Just as his moral theory takes on a new religious

[15] *Handbook*, p. 202.

orientation in *Christmas-Eve and Easter-Day*, his aesthetic theory is redefined in complementary terms in the *Essay on Shelley*.

Browning's *Essay on Shelley* was written in 1851 and withdrawn from circulation immediately after the letters of Shelley which it introduced were discovered to be spurious. Although the book was suppressed, Browning's *Essay* is generally recognized as an important document in the history of his thought, particularly because it is his only extant formal prose work, with the exception of his short prefaces, which deals explicitly with poetic theory. Until recently, the *Essay* has been accepted as a fairly straightforward exercise in which Browning first defines a set of poetic terms that were in current use in the mid-nineteenth century—"objective" and "subjective"—and then applies them to specific individuals—Shakespeare and Shelley—for the purpose of extolling Shelley's merits as an exemplar of the subjective mode. According to this point of view, Browning sees himself as a subjective-objective poet. The accuracy of this standard interpretation, presented by W. C. DeVane in his *Browning Handbook*,[16] has, however, been challenged by Philip Drew in his article "Browning's *Essay on Shelley*."[17] Drew contends that if the essay is read carefully, it becomes clear that Browning does not identify Shelley as a subjective poet, but rather that he regards Shelley as one who successfully combines the objective and subjective roles, and that he sees himself as an objective poet. Another dissenter, Mrs. Betty Miller, claims that Browning actually deprecates the so-called objective poet, and in so doing is deprecating himself.[18]

The point of major interest here is not which of these readings is correct, but why it is that three critics could read the same short prose essay and come up with three different opinions as to its meaning. The contention to which the *Essay* has given rise is perhaps the best clue we have to reading it correctly—a clue which, it seems, no one has yet discovered because of a reticence to admit that even in prose Browning is as inconsistent and ambiguous as he frequently is in poetry. Thus it

[16] Pp. 577–580. With respect to Browning's attitude toward Shelley, DeVane writes that in the *Essay* "Shelley represents the 'subjective' poet, *par excellence* . . ." (p. 578). Alba H. Warren also erroneously labels Shelley as Browning's example of the subjective poet. See his *English Poetic Theory: 1825–1865* (Princeton: Princeton University Press, 1950), p. 122.

[17] *Victorian Poetry*, I (January 1963), 1–6.

[18] *Portrait*, p. 173.

is helpful to sort out and examine the inconsistencies and ambiguities in the *Essay*, and attempt to resolve them by considering it in relationship to the poetry discussed in this and preceding chapters. What emerges from such a consideration is that Browning, by converting Shelley from the atheistic utopian of *Pauline* and *Paracelsus* to a religiously inspired humanist, by attributing to his onetime mentor a belief (or at least a potential belief) in Christianity and the Incarnation, by praising him as a "whole poet" who possesses both objective and subjective powers, is not really talking about Shelley at all, but projecting into the name and person of Shelley the ideals and aspirations which he himself had assimilated by 1851.[19] From the *Essay*, as somewhat less explicitly from *Christmas-Eve and Easter-Day*, Browning emerges as a Christian "whole poet." But in the *Essay*, and quite contradictory to his earlier poetic statements, these are the qualities he attributes to Shelley.

Browning begins the *Essay* by defining and distinguishing between the terms "objective" and "subjective."[20] The objective poet is one who reproduces external phenomena in such a way that the creation will be beneficial to his audience: "to reproduce things external . . . with an immediate reference, in every case, to the common eye and apprehension of his fellow-men, assumed capable of receiving and profiting by this reproduction." This method of reproduction requires a double talent on the part of the poet. He must see "external objects more clearly, widely, and deeply than is possible to the average mind," and at the same time he must have the ability to organize and communicate his apprehension in such a manner that those who do not

[19] Mrs. Miller recognizes this self-projection on Browning's part, but does not explore it fully or, I think, accurately. See *Portrait*, p. 174.

[20] These terms were popularized by Kant, and became part of the English critical vocabulary in the second decade of the nineteenth century. See Meyer H. Abrams, *The Mirror and the Lamp* (Norton Library ed.; New York: W. W. Norton, 1958), pp. 235–244, for a detailed account of their transposition into the English. Browning's casual introduction of them (the objective poet "as the phrase now goes," and the subjective poet "of modern classification") indicates that they were commonly accepted critical parlance as late as 1850. The terms and the duality of poetic endeavor they signify are discussed at length in the *R.B.–E.B.B.* correspondence of 1845–1846, as will be shown later in this chapter. Citations from the *Essay on Shelley* are from the most accessible text, in *The Complete Poetical Works of Browning*, ed. Horace E. Scudder (Cambridge ed.; Boston: Houghton Mifflin, 1895), pp. 1008–1014. Since the *Essay* is so short, I have not cited page references after each quotation.

see as deeply as he will understand what he is attempting to say. Although Browning here seems to imply that the objective poet writes down to his audience,[21] he does not mean that the poet's skill in reorganizing and amplifying his material excludes those who are able to comprehend more than the average man. Since he has a double talent, of both perception and expression, the objective poet must also have a double audience: those who have the ability to recreate his perceptions and those who passively accept them at their face value. In both cases, fresh knowledge of external reality may be gained: "The auditory of such a poet will include, not only the intelligences which, save for such assistance, would have missed the deeper meaning and enjoyment of the original objects, but also the spirits of a like endowment with his own, who, by means of his abstract, can forthwith pass to the reality it was made from, and either corroborate their impressions of things known already, or supply themselves with new from whatever shows in the inexhaustible variety of existence may have hitherto escaped their knowledge." Such a poet is called a "fashioner"; and because his poetry will be "projected from himself and distinct," a knowledge of his life is not necessary for the understanding of his work. The prime example of a fashioner is Shakespeare.

Whereas the objective poet organizes his perceptions with regard for the limitations of his audience, the subjective poet, or "seer," is "impelled to embody the thing he perceives, not so much with reference to the many below as to the one above him, the supreme Intelligence which apprehends all things in their absolute truth,—an ultimate view ever aspired to, if but partially attained, by the poet's own soul. Not what man sees, but what God sees,—the *Ideas* of Plato, seeds of creation lying burningly on the Divine Hand,—it is toward these that he struggles." Browning goes on to explain that the essential difference between the two poets is not so much in their methods of perception as in the adaptability of the materials they employ.[22] The objective poet appeals to the "aggregate human mind," and so depicts the actions of men. Conversely, the subjective poet, who appeals to the "absolute Divine mind," dwells on external appearances which serve to draw forth his own "inner light and power."

[21] Warren, *English Poetic Theory*, p. 117.
[22] *Ibid.*, p. 119.

Having made these initial distinctions, Browning then proceeds to evaluate the relative worth of the two positions. He admits the validity and necessity of both kinds of poetry, but he is slightly defensive with respect to the position of the fashioner:

> It would be idle to inquire, of these two kinds of poetic faculty in operation, which is the higher or even rarer endowment. If the subjective might seem to be the ultimate requirement of every age, the objective, in the strictest state, must still retain its original value. For it is with this world, as starting point and basis alike, that we shall always have to concern ourselves: the world is not to be learned and thrown aside, but reverted to and relearned. The spiritual comprehension may be infinitely subtilized, but the raw material it operates upon must remain.

This statement is not "condemnatory" of the role of the objective poet, as Mrs. Miller contends, nor is it true that because Browning defends this position he is necessarily defending himself. The poet is here simply reasserting ideas which formed the nucleus of *Paracelsus* and *Sordello*: that the finite exhibitions of nature are not to be ignored, but used as "the starting point and basis alike" of artistic endeavor. Similarly, the qualifications Browning states in the *Essay* concerning the idealistic and visionary goal of the subjective poet are carried over from his earlier work. Although the subjective poet is called a "seer," he is not granted that absolute vision of truth which is his goal. That "ultimate view" is "ever aspired to, if but partially attained, by the poet's own soul." The seer's struggles are but partially rewarded: "An absolute vision is not for this world, but we are permitted a continual approximation to it . . . ."

Before turning to a discussion of Shelley, Browning enumerates the various ways in which the two approaches to poetry have been practiced in the past, and points to his personal preference by suggesting that the best poetry is that which fuses the objective and subjective modes. His prose is rather involved in this section of the *Essay*, but Browning seems to be saying that until the mid-nineteenth century the two kinds of poetry have been written by different individuals: "Nor is there any reason why these two modes of poetic faculty may not issue hereafter from the same poet in successive perfect works, examples of which, according to what are now considered the exigencies of art, we have hitherto possessed in distinct individuals only." He then qualifies the second half of this statement by explaining on the one hand that occasionally the two faculties are inadequately fused—"a mere running in of the one faculty upon the other is, of course, the ordinary circumstance"—and, on the other, that instances of either a purely objective or a purely subjective poet are literary rarities: "Far more rarely it happens that either is found so decidedly prominent and superior as to be pronounced comparatively pure...." Finally, he returns to his original argument, reasserting that the best poetry would combine subjectivity and objectivity, and that such a fusion has never been achieved: "while of the perfect shield, with the gold and the silver side set up for all comers to challenge, there has yet been no instance."

Up to this point, the *Essay on Shelley* is reasonably clear. The terms have been defined, one of them has been applied to Shakespeare, and the reader knows that in Browning's opinion English literature has not produced an artist who is capable of brandishing a "perfect shield." Without reading further, the inevitable conclusion would be the one drawn by DeVane—that Shelley will now be cited as the subjective poet who dealt, or tried to deal, with the "*Ideas* of Plato." This conclusion would be wholly consistent with Browning's allusions to Shelley in his earlier poetry, as are the qualifying remarks mentioned above regarding such a poet's frustrating "struggles" toward the ultimate. Here again we would have a perfect description not only of Shelley, but of the hero of *Pauline*, Aprile, Paracelsus, Sordello, and the young Robert Browning. But Browning now contradicts these ideas enunciated in his youthful poetry, and he even appears to forget that he has unequivocally stated in the *Essay* itself that there has never been an adequate fusion of the seer-fashioner roles. Shelley has, by some incomprehensible transformation, become a "whole poet."[23]

Browning writes that while it is necessary to know the biography of the subjective poet in order to fully understand his work, it is only because Shelley died in his youth, and because his life has since been misunderstood and falsified, that biography is helpful in his case. Like the objective poet, Shelley's personality shines forth from his poetry. Under usual circumstances his work alone would be a sufficient

---

[23] Browning's view of Shelley as a "whole poet" is discussed by Drew. However, Drew sees nothing inconsistent in this appraisal, either within the *Essay* or in relationship to Browning's poetry of the 1830's. He dismisses the second half of the *Essay*, in which Browning defends Shelley, as "of no immediate interest" (p. 3); it is, nevertheless, extremely interesting and important.

reflection of his thought: "We must in every case betake ourselves to the review of a [subjective] poet's life ere we determine some of the nicer questions concerning his poetry .... I concede, however, in respect to this subject of our study ... that the unmistakable quality of the verse would be evidence enough, under usual circumstances, not only of the kind and degree of the intellectual but of the moral constitution of Shelley; the whole personality of the poet shining forward from the poems, without much need of going further to seek it." And the personality which shines forth from Shelley's work is that of a fashioner-seer: the gold and silver shield embodying the fusion of elements, dramatic and lyric, actual and ideal, natural and spiritual, which according to Browning's definitions are the proper spheres of the objective and subjective poets respectively: "The 'Remains' ... [are] examples, in fact, of the whole poet's function of beholding with an understanding keenness the universe, nature and man, in their actual state of perfection in imperfection; of the whole poet's virtue of being untempted, by the manifold partial developments of beauty and good on every side, into leaving them the ultimates he found them ...." Shelley, whose "spheric poetical faculty" possesses "its own self-sacrificing central light," has, in Browning's estimation, no artistic equal:

> ... his simultaneous perception of Power and Love in the absolute, and of Beauty and Good in the concrete, while he throws, from his poet's station between both, swifter, subtler, and more numerous films for the connection of each with each, than have been thrown by any modern artificer of whom I have knowledge ....
>
> I would rather consider Shelley's poetry as a sublime fragmentary essay towards a presentment of the correspondency of the universe to Deity, of the natural to the spiritual, and of the actual to the ideal, than I would isolate and separately appraise the worth of many detachable portions which might be acknowledged as utterly perfect in a lower moral point of view, under the mere conditions of art.

This is not the Shelley of *Pauline* and *Paracelsus*. The "Sun-treader," the poet who aspires to infinite love, has become a perfect poet who fuses the natural and the spiritual, the actual and the ideal. But is it Shelley or Browning who has undergone a transformation? It becomes increasingly clear in the second half of the *Essay* that although Shelley is the ostensible subject of Browning's discussion, the poet is talking, however obliquely, about himself and what he would like his own poetry to accomplish. Shelley becomes simply one more means, along with the figure of Christ, Evangelical religion, and the concept of Christian love in *Christmas-Eve and Easter-Day*, through which Browning envisages the reconciliation of the real with the ideal. There is sufficient evidence, both in the *Essay* and in Browning's other writings, to support this claim.

Before we turn to the evidence available in Browning's own work, it should be noted that in the *Essay*, both when he defines the terms "objective" and "subjective" and when he praises Shelley, the "whole poet," Browning closely echoes a number of statements made by Elizabeth Barrett about his own work and applies them to Shelley. Since the terms "objective" and "subjective" were in current use in the 1840's, it is hardly surprising to find Elizabeth Barrett employing them. But the affinity between her statements about Browning and Browning's statements about Shelley is extremely suggestive. It is equally curious that no one has yet noted as particularly significant the fact that these obvious parallels exist. It is generally agreed that Elizabeth Barrett helped Browning with his religious difficulties, and her stylistic influence has been thoroughly documented.[24] The following excerpts from the love letters suggest that perhaps she deserves more credit for the maturation of Browning's aesthetic theory than has hitherto been acknowledged, even if we are willing to concede only that her chief contribution was in bringing into an articulate focus, and applying to Browning, a number of critical terms and ideas which were frequently employed, in a diversity of ways, by poetic theoreticians during this period.

> Why should you deny the full measure of my delight and benefit from your writings? I could tell you why you should not. You have in your vision *two worlds*, or to use the language of the schools of the day, *you are both subjective and objective* in the habits of your mind. You can deal both with *abstract thought* and with *human passion* in the most passionate sense. Thus, you have an immense grasp in Art; and no one at all accustomed to

[24] See the following for comments on Elizabeth Barrett's stylistic influence: J. W. Cunliffe, "Elizabeth Barrett's Influence on Browning's Poetry," *PMLA*, XXIII (June 1908), 169–183; Bernice Fox, "Revision In Browning's *Paracelsus*," *Modern Language Notes*, LV (March 1940), 195–197; *New Poems by Robert Browning and Elizabeth Barrett Browning*, ed. F. G. Kenyon (London: Smith, Elder, 1914), pp. 140–176; Edward Snyder and Frederic Palmer, Jr., "New Light on the Brownings," *Quarterly Review*, CCLXIX (1937), 48–63.

consider the usual forms of it, could help regarding with reverence and
gladness the gradual expansion of your powers.[25]

You have taken a *great range*—from those *high faint notes of the mystics*
which are beyond personality . . to *dramatic impersonations* . . . and
when these are thrown into *harmony*, as in a manner they are in "Pippa
Passes" . . . the *combinations of effect* must always be striking and noble—
and you must feel yourself drawn on to such *combinations* more and
more.[26]

For it is quite startling, I must tell you, quite startling and humiliating, to
observe how you *combine* such large tracts of experience of *outer and inner
life . . . curious knowledge* as well as *general knowledge* . . and *deep thinking*
as well as *wide acquisition* . . . .[27]

Why it is full of hope for both of us, to look forward and consider what
you may achieve with that *combination* of *authority over* the *reasons* and the
*passions*, and that wonderful *variety* of the *plastic power*![28]

And what a triumph (after all!) and what a privilege, and what a good
deed, is this carrying of the light down into the mines among the work-
men, this bringing down of the *angels* of the *Ideal* into the very *depth* of
the *Real*, where the hammer rings on the rough stone.[29]

Browning's poetry before 1851 substantiates the suspicion to which
these letters give rise—that in the *Essay* Browning is identifying
Shelley with himself.

[25] January 15, 1845, *Letters of R.B. and E.B.B.*, I, 8. Italics in this and the
following letters are mine.
[26] February 17, 1845, *ibid.*, I, 22. The two-point ellipses are in the original letter.
[27] August 20, 1845, *ibid.*, I, 168.
[28] March 30, 1846, *ibid.*, II, 14.
[29] April 22, 1846, *ibid.*, II, 92. There is no doubt that in 1845 and 1846 Browning
needed all this encouragement. Not only was he dissatisfied with *Bells and Pomegranates*, but at this time, possibly because of *Bells* and "Saul," he understandably
lacked confidence in the value of his own poetic ability. His frequently quoted
complaints that he fears "the pure white light" and can only give truth "broken
into prismatic hues" (January 13, 1845, *R.B. and E.B.B.*, I, 6), and that he cannot
write "'R.B. a poem'" (February 11, 1845, I, 17), are, however, not particularly
surprising when these frustrations at his inability to write "whole" poetry are seen
in the context of his earlier work. His complaints, and her encouragement, again
illustrate that in 1845–1846 Browning had not yet solved the moral and aesthetic
problems which then confronted him. On the positive side, the interchanges
between the two correspondents prove that he had not given up trying to solve
them.

As I have shown in the preceding chapters, Browning's poetry before the *Essay* reflects a constant preoccupation with defining in workable terms the duality with which the *Essay on Shelley* and the above-mentioned letters are so concerned. In *Pauline* the poles of interest were Shelley and God—atheism and utopianism, faith and practicality. *Paracelsus* dwelt upon the philosophic implications of reconciling the finite with the infinite, while in *Sordello* the same subject was treated in terms of aesthetics. Ostensibly, the conflict was solved in *Sordello*, but Browning's inability to complete "Saul" in 1845 points to his deficiency at that time in translating theory into practice. He was incapable of completing the poem because he was not yet certain about the validity of transcending the fashioner's role he had so arduously cultivated in his dramatic efforts between 1836 and 1845. In *Christmas-Eve and Easter-Day*, written immediately before the *Essay*, we see Browning formulating, this time in a Christian context, the same antithetical terms treated in *Paracelsus* and *Sordello*. The person of Christ in the Incarnation comes to represent for Browning in *Christmas-Eve and Easter-Day* the reconciliation of the actual and the ideal, the imperfect and the perfect.

Significantly, in the *Essay on Shelley*, Browning's rationale for calling Shelley a "whole poet" rests upon the strikingly coincidental fact that Shelley was potentially capable of the conversion Browning illustrates as his own experience in *Christmas-Eve and Easter-Day*. Some time after 1845, Browning adopted a belief in Christ, in the Incarnation, and in Christianity. So, it seems, did Shelley, or at least Browning says he would have if he had lived longer:

> Gradually he was raised above the contemplation of spots and the attempt at effacing them, to the great Abstract Light, and through the discrepancy of the creation, to the sufficiency of the First Cause. Gradually he was learning that the best way of removing abuses is to stand fast by truth . . . .
> I shall say what I think,—had Shelley lived he would have finally ranged himself with the Christians . . . . The preliminary step to following Christ, is the leaving the dead to bury their dead—not clamoring on his doctrine for an especial solution of difficulties which are referable to the general problem of the universe.

According to Browning, evidence of Shelley's Christian leanings is illustrated by a passage from "The Boat on the Serchio," in which a belief in the all-important Incarnation is suggested:

"All rose to do the task He set to each,
Who shaped us to His ends and not our own;
The million rose to learn, and One to teach
What none yet ever knew or can be known."

And this, Browning triumphantly proclaims, is similar to the discovery made by another poet long ago, a poet who posed a major difficulty for Browning himself in 1845: "No more difference than this, from David's pregnant conclusion so long ago!"

With this declaration, Browning has come the full circle back to "Saul." By employing the religious convictions gained after 1846, and by fusing, in the poet David, the roles of the objective and subjective poets, Browning could now complete "Saul" and unleash the full potential of his talent for the major poetic achievement in *Men and Women, Dramatis Personae*, and *The Ring and the Book*.

The 1845 version of "Saul" ends at the ninth stanza with the poet David praising King Saul as the epitome of creation. In those nine stanzas, David has worked through the various levels of existence, beginning with inanimate stones and waters, progressing to the animate level of cricket and jerboa, then to the reaper, and finally to Saul himself. With this attempt by the poet to revive Saul with a song which is based on purely physical phenomena, David may be said to have fulfilled the role later assigned by Browning in the *Essay* to the objective poet: he has used the world of material reality as "the starting point and basis alike" of successful poetry. In the stanzas added after Browning wrote the *Essay*, David, rising above the natural order, achieves the insight of the subjective poet in the redemptive vision of the Incarnation. Browning indicates, through David's fusion of these poetic roles, that he now understands not only the necessity, but also the means, by which Saul can be offered spiritual consolation. As noted in the *Essay*, the value of art rests upon the artist's ability to emcompass both "raw material" and "spiritual comprehension" in his work.

David's—and therefore Browning's—awareness of the transition which must take place in the subject matter of his song becomes clear in stanzas ten, eleven, and twelve, in which he meditates on the problems that confront him with regard to Saul's spiritual regeneration. Thus far the cure is only half completed. The naturalistic celebration of the material joys of life and manhood have reanimated Saul's physical sensitivity:

> One long shudder thrilled
> All the tent till the very air tingled, then
> sank and was stilled,
> At the King's self left standing before me,
> released and aware,
>
> (pp. 123–124)[30]

but he is still spiritually numb: "Death was past, life not come" (p. 124).

The poet knows that if his song is to have any effect on Saul, the King must understand the nature of the song itself and, consequently, the purpose of poetic transition from objective to subjective insight. In stanza thirteen David, through the use of the palm tree metaphor, explains why a successful poet must be both objective and subjective with respect to his subject matter:

> "In our flesh grows the branch of this life, in our
> soul it bears fruit.
>
> .  .  .  .  .  .  .  .  .  .  .  .
>
> Our dates shall we slight,
> When their juice brings a cure for all sorrow? or
> care for the plight
> Of the palm's self whose slow growth produced them?
> Not so! stem and branch
> Shall decay, nor be known in their place, while
> the palm-wine shall staunch
> Every wound of man's spirit in winter. I pour
> thee such wine.
> Leave the flesh to the fate it was fit for! the spirit
> be thine!
>
> .  .  .  .  .  .  .  .  .  .  .  .  .
>
> Thou hast done now with eyes for the actual; begin
> with the seer's!"
>
> (pp. 127–130)

The eyes of the fashioner, who describes the "actual," are necessary; but now poet and listener must "begin with the seer's!"

---

[30] Quotations from "Saul" are from Robert Browning's *Men and Women* (London, 1855), II, 111–146. Since the lines in this edition are unnumbered, page numbers are cited following quotations.

In order to achieve this movement to the vision of the seer, David commences a song which describes the spiritual accomplishments Saul has enjoyed in the past or will enjoy in the future. It is not, however, until David has ended his song that the truth breaks upon him:

> "'Tis the weakness in strength that I cry
> for! my flesh, that I seek
> In the Godhead! I seek and I find it. O
> Saul, it shall be
> A Face like my face that receives thee: a
> Man like to me,
> Thou shall love and be loved by, for ever!
> a Hand like this hand
> Shall throw open the gates of new life to
> thee! See the Christ stand!"

(p. 144)

In relation to the subject matter of the poem, David's prophetic vision of the Incarnation represents the final step—and the climax—of the progressive development noted above. David the fashioner informs Saul first of physical truth, and then, in his movement to the role of the subjective poet or seer, of spiritual truth. The Incarnation, Christ as God-man, unites the dual strains of the poem in a perfect harmony. It signifies not only the ultimate spiritual understanding inherent in the perception of the poet, but also combines both aspects of the poet's vision. The Incarnation as image becomes the link in joining the powers of the objective and subjective poets. Christ as the union of flesh and spirit appeals to both the "aggregate human mind" and the "absolute Divine mind."

"Saul," then, may be considered the conscious working out of the moral-aesthetic theories explored by Browning in *Christmas-Eve and Easter-Day* and the *Essay on Shelley*. It represents the successful conclusion and, in a necessarily compressed form, a summary of the major moral and aesthetic theories developed by Browning after the obstructions which faced him in 1845. It also signifies a new beginning: Browning was now ready for his *Men and Women*.

## CHAPTER SIX

# *Men and Women*: Culmination

*Men and Women* represents the culmination of Robert Browning's moral-aesthetic development. But because the over-all quality of the verse contained in *Men and Women* is so high, and because so much of his early work is distinctly inferior, readers of Browning have tended to treat his mature poems as isolated units which fully illustrate the poet's strength both as a technician and as a thinker, while de-emphasizing the fact that his best work is the inevitable result of years of struggle to achieve technical perfection and moral-aesthetic ideological certainty. Recently, however, Park Honan has discussed the continuity of technique which connects the early poetry to the mature monologues.[1]

[1] *Browning's Characters: A Study in Poetic Technique* (New Haven: Yale University Press, 1961). See also C. Willard Smith's, *Browning's Star-Imagery* (Princeton: Princeton University Press, 1941), an informative study of one important imagistic pattern in Browning's poetry. Several important aspects of Browning's aesthetic theory are fulfilled through the "technical" achievement Honan discusses. Because their initial formulation occurs in *Sordello*, they are worth recalling here, since they add to our awareness that Browning's best poetry is the fruition of thoughts he had entertained some years before. Indeed, they were pointed out in Chapter Three precisely because although critics clearly discern Browning's methods in the dramatic monologue (and in Honan's case the development of a method), they fail to recognize that Browning first discusses their theoretical validity in the irksome *Sordello*. For example, Honan's detailed treatment of style explains what happened during the period of Browning's dedication to drama to the "brother's speech" discussed in *Sordello*. The language, and the handling of language, in the dramatic monologue is used by Browning to reveal character. This is accomplished, in part, by intonation, repetition, suggestion of ideas through connotation, and rhythmic variation—all of which contribute to the effect suggested in *Sordello*: "speech where an accent's change gives each / The other's Soul." Also, the desire to delineate character and to reveal a wide spectrum of human moral conditions, both of which are immediate concerns of the dramatic monologue, are foreshadowed in *Sordello* by the poet's desire to "read profound / Disclosures" in a person's face, by his dedication to Humanity and to the problem of evil. Another accomplishment in the dramatic monologue is Browning's ability to draw the reader into the poem. Robert Langbaum's explanation of a reader's

Likewise, a survey of the moral-aesthetic theory expressed in *Men and Women* shows that the ideas Browning articulates in this group of poems are the outgrowth and, in a sense, a summary of the theory developed in his work up through the *Essay on Shelley*. The establishment of this continuity, already briefly suggested in my discussion of "Saul," which was itself published in *Men and Women*, is a logical conclusion to a study of the development of Browning's moral-aesthetic ideas.

"Saul" is, as I have indicated, the epitome of Browning's moral-aesthetic philosophy. Begun in 1845, published in its entirety as one of the fifty men and women in 1855, and drawing so directly on the *Essay on Shelley* and the period of development which its composition covers, "Saul" is the most obvious connecting link between the ideas formulated by Browning up to 1851 and those set forth in *Men and Women*. Through David's vision of the Incarnation, the poem brings together the most important of Browning's theoretical principles concerning love, religion, and art. David as objective-subjective poet fuses the infinite and the finite in the symbol of Christ. As moralist, or spiritual guide to Saul, he advocates the acceptance of Christ as the means through which Saul can attain spiritual wholeness. He is successful in both roles because he understands the principle of Divine love, and its human counterpart, both of which are manifested through the Incarnation and which Browning had discussed in such detail in *Christmas-Eve and Easter-Day*. By synthesizing these three elements, "Saul" not only reflects the major areas of Browning's investigations prior to 1851, but it also points to the subjects of major importance in its companion poems in *Men and Women*. Love, religion, and art are the predominant themes in *Men and Women*, just as they are in *Christmas-Eve and Easter-Day* and the *Essay on Shelley*.[2]

---

involvement in the poetry through the engagement of sympathy (*The Poetry of Experience* [London: Chatto and Windus, 1957]) is an amplification of Browning's own statement, "Yourselves effect what I was fain before / Effect, what I supplied yourselves suggest, / What I leave bare yourselves can now invest." Finally, by reading both Langbaum and Honan one can see how Browning combines lyric and dramatic techniques in the dramatic monologue to effect a judicious compromise between the two poetic forms. In *Sordello*, Browning states his preference for synthetic poetry over drama, but it is not surprising to note that after his years of writing drama following *Sordello*, he employs dramatic methods to write synthetic poetry. He becomes, as so many critics have stated, both dramatic and lyrical.

[2] William Whitla's *The Central Truth: The Incarnation in Browning's Poetry*

And it is the continuity of thought that Browning's treatment of these themes reveals which justifies the contention that *Men and Women* represents the culmination of Browning's moral-aesthetic development.

## OF LOVE

Browning's early poetry is concerned chiefly with an investigation of the condition which exists when love is either neglected or imperfectly realized. The hero of *Pauline*, Paracelsus, Aprile, and Sordello suffer in varying degrees from the malady which results when love, that quality which inseparably joins two human beings, or a human being to God, is unfulfilled. Resolutions are reached in *Pauline* and *Paracelsus* only after the major characters have dedicated themselves to God through the love of finite creation: the hero of *Pauline* acknowledges the sanative influence of nature and asserts his dedication to the imaginary Pauline, and Paracelsus finally comes to understand his error in divorcing himself from humanity. But although each poem definitely states the value of sharing in human love, the true function of the ideal relationship which should exist between a man and a woman is not fully explained until *Sordello*. In this poem, through the Sordello-Palma relationship, Browning formulates the ideas which not only inform the conception of love enunciated in his later poetry, but which also prophetically point to the role that Elizabeth Barrett was soon to play in his own life.

In Book Six of the poem, when Sordello ponders the question of how to "order Life" (VI.575), Browning intrudes to offer a solution: "Ah my Sordello, I this once befriend / And speak for you" (VI.592–593). Browning explains that although man must believe in a Divine Being, he should not attempt to achieve direct access to one who is so far beyond his comprehension. Instead, he must establish a relationship

---

(Toronto: University of Toronto Press, 1963), traces these themes in some detail through Browning's mature poetry. While Whitla's discussion of individual poems is frequently cogent and convincing, the work as a whole suffers from his attempt to impose a trinitarian pattern on all of Browning's poetry. Whitla's conclusion points to the major deficiency of his own position: "In the present resurgence of Browning studies in examinations of Victorian poetry, it would be wise to be creative rather than destructive ... to seek for poetic principles like harmony, unity, wholeness of vision, rather than fragmentation, duality, and conflict" (pp. 153–154). Such distinctions are invalid. Surely it is only because of the fragmentation, duality, and conflict of Browning's early work that the poetry written after 1852 can be spoken of in terms of its harmony and unity.

with another human who is, for him, representative of God on earth—one who could most effectively direct him to that "out-Nature" (VI.598):

> a Power its representative
> Who, being for authority the same,
> Communication different, should claim
> A course the first chose and this last revealed—
> This Human clear, as that Divine concealed.
>
> (VI.600–604)

Sordello is, of course, a poet, and hence this "out-soul" (III.314) is seen not only as an object of love, an intermediary who possesses the power to perfect Sordello the man's contact with God, but also as a potential source of inspiration for Sordello the poet. Had Sordello realized his love for Palma, she could have become the "moon" which was required to stir the "sea-depths" of his poetic nature:

> Demanding only outward influence,
> A soul, in Palma's phrase, above his soul,
> Power to uplift his power, this moon's control,
> Over the sea-depths
>
> . . . . . . . . . . .
>                 but years and years the sky above
> Held none, and so, untasked of any love,
> His sensitiveness idled.
>
> (VI.41–48)

Five years after the publication of *Sordello*, Browning met Elizabeth Barrett, who played an important role in activating his religious as well as poetic sensitivity. The tribute he pays to her in *Men and Women* is doubly interesting, for he not only explicitly acknowledges her influence in the dedicatory "One Word More" and the deeply personal "By the Fireside" in terminology reminiscent of that employed in *Sordello*, but he uses the understanding gained through the perfection of their love as a basis on which to write poems that range from the depiction of completely harmonious love in "Love Among the Ruins," to its partial fulfillment in "Two in the Campagna" and "The Last Ride Together," to its absolute negation in "A Serenade at the Villa." Taken as a group, these poems offer a representative survey of Browning's analysis of the degrees of human love in *Men and Women*, and clearly reiterate the importance of love as set forth in *Christmas-Eve and Easter-Day* and "Saul": love is the agent which allows man to use, and yet also rise above, the flesh which binds him to the finite.

In "One Word More" and "By the Fireside" Browning acknowledges his debt to Elizabeth Barrett Browning. She is his Palma, the moon who has stirred the sea-depths of his poetic sensitivity, the intermediary through whom he has successfully attained access to the "out-Nature" who is God. The poet explains in "One Word More" that although Rafael and Dante were able to honor their loved ones by "Using nature that's an art to others" (II, 233)[3]—by forsaking their own mediums of expression and employing arts in which they were relatively unaccomplished—he can only stand on his "attainment. / This of verse alone, one life allows me" (II, 236). And through verse he gives himself and his art totally into her possession:

> Pray you, look on these my men and women,
> Take and keep my fifty poems finished;
> Where my heart lies, let my brain lie also!
>
> (II, 237–238)

Browning does not explicitly state that it is as a result of his lover's inspiration that he has been successful in creating these men and women, but in the parallel drawn between their love and that of Dante and Beatrice, and in his acknowledgment of Elizabeth as his "moon of poets" (II, 240), Browning delineates his feelings of gratitude with unmistakable clarity.[4] And it is significant that while Browning proclaims the ultimate triumph of his love, he recognizes at the same time the imperfection of the very form which he employs to celebrate that achievement: "Poor the speech; be how I speak, for all things" (II, 238).

While "One Word More" acknowledges Elizabeth's influence on Browning's art, "By the Fireside" may be read as an expression of Browning's thanks for his wife's contribution to his religious development. This poem describes the moment of perfectly realized love, as well as its meaning. The speaker in "By the Fireside" imagines

---

[3] All citations in this chapter are from Robert Browning's *Men and Women* (2 vols.; London, 1855). Since the lines in this edition are unnumbered, page numbers are cited following quotations.

[4] The moon imagery is mentioned by W. C. DeVane, *A Browning Handbook* (2d ed.; New York: Appleton-Century-Crofts, 1955), p. 278.

himself reminiscing over past events as he sits by the hearth "In life's November" (I, 63) with his wife, his perfect Leonor. They are silent, but the union they have achieved through love enables them to communicate by means of mutual intuitive understanding:

> When, if I think but deep enough,
> You are wont to answer, prompt as rhyme;
> And you, too, find without a rebuff
> The response your soul seeks many a time
> Piercing its fine flesh-stuff.
>
> (I, 71)

Mentally the narrator retraces the path of their love to the time when it first became an actuality—to that instant in the woods when the complete blending of their souls produced the supreme "moment, one and infinite!" (I, 75). It was at this "infinite moment," the speaker declares, that the course his life would take thereafter was unalterably determined:

> I am named and known by that hour's feat,
> There took my station and degree.
> So grew my own small life complete
> As nature obtained her best of me—
> One born to love you, sweet!
>
> (I, 80)

But even more important to the narrator, and to Browning himself, than the "infinite moment" and its consequence of fixing his course in life is the fact that the lovers have pierced the "mortal screen" of life by allowing themselves to move with nature's rhythms, by utilizing the imperfect means at their disposal to overcome the barrier of flesh which separates them:

> A moment after, and hands unseen
> Were hanging the night around us fast.
> But we knew that a bar was broken between
> Life and life; we were mixed at last
> In spite of the mortal screen.
> The forests had done it; there they stood—
> We caught for a second the powers at play:
> They had mingled us so, for once and for good,
> Their work was done.
>
> (I, 78–79)

And this experience has resulted in a spiritual maturity which brings the two souls, now each "sucked / Into each" (I, 71), closer to God:

> Think, when our one soul understands
> The great Word which makes all things new—
> When earth breaks up and Heaven expands—
> How will the change strike me and you
> In the House not made with hands?
> Oh, I must feel your brain prompt mine,
> Your heart anticipate my heart,
> You must be just before, in fine,
> See and make me see, for your part,
> New depths of the Divine!
>
> (I, 72)

Seen in the context of Browning's advice to Sordello, this last stanza, and the reference to Elizabeth Barrett Browning as "moon" in "One Word More," would seem to be deliberate indications on Browning's part that through his love for his wife, his "out-soul," he has succeeded where Sordello failed. The way to the infinite is through the finite, and human love is the power through which this movement is to be effected.

There is one additional poem in *Men and Women*, "Love Among the Ruins," which also has as its theme "love realized," and it deserves notice here because in it Browning examines, in language similar to that used in *Easter-Day*, the value of love as compared to that of other earthly accomplishments. It will be remembered that the narrator in *Easter-Day* chooses love after he has considered and been directed to discount the ultimate value of nature, art, and reason. "Love Among the Ruins" illustrates, through a use of the same comparative method, Browning's estimation of love's supremacy.

The male speaker of "Love Among the Ruins" stands observing the countryside with its "Miles and miles" of "solitary pastures" (I, 1), and reflects that at one point in history this serene and almost desolate land was the site of a "city great and gay" (I, 1). Where there once stood a magnificent castle surrounded by a marble wall, there is now only a single turret "By the caper overrooted, by the gourd / Overscored" (I, 4). The grandeur of an empire has been destroyed, but for him the dingy ruined tower holds more than an empire could for a monarch—"a girl with eager eyes and yellow hair / Waits me there" (I, 5).

The ruler of that once great city looked out from the tower upon the transitory splendor of material things, on nature and the embellishments added to nature by man's ingenuity:

> he looked upon the city, every side,
> Far and wide,
> All the mountains topped with temples, all the glades'
> Colonnades,
> All the causeys, bridges, aqueducts,—and then,
> All the men!
>
> (I, 5)

The lovers, in contrast, will look only inward, at one another:

> When I do come, she will speak not, she will stand,
> Either hand
> On my shoulder, give her eyes the first embrace
> Of my face,
> Ere we rush, ere we extinguish sight and speech
> Each on each.
>
> (I, 5–6)

The relative values of an empire based on material wealth and power and one based on the love of a single individual for another are incomparable:

> Oh, heart! oh, blood that freezes, blood that burns!
> Earth's returns
> For whole centuries of folly, noise and sin!
> Shut them in,
> With their triumphs and their glories and the rest.
> Love is best!
>
> (I, 6)

The conclusion reached in "Love Among the Ruins" is as positive, and as unmistakably Browning's, as that of *Easter-Day*. The triumphant lover sees clearly that men die, that wealth and power are transitory. Standing amid the ruins of all that is symbolic of purely material endeavor, he proclaims that "Love is best!" because he knows that it is the only means accessible to man which can lift him beyond the decay that invariably infects and destroys the debris of tainted human existence.

A similar judgment is expressed in "The Last Ride Together," which has as its theme the superiority of love to poetry, sculpture, and music. The difference between this poem and those discussed above is that Browning here depicts a rejected lover. However, even the partial satisfaction the narrator experiences when his mistress lays her head on his breast, "Thus leant she and lingered—joy and fear! / Thus lay she a moment on my breast" (I, 186), is, for him, a sufficiently realized "infinite moment." For a second his being is completed, and it is important to note that the occasion is again described by Browning in terms of "moon" and "heaven":

> And so, you, looking and loving best,
> Conscious grew, your passion drew
> Cloud, sunset, moonrise, star-shine too
> Down on you, near and yet more near,
> Till flesh must fade for heaven was here!
>
> (I, 186)

The ardent suitor and the lover who has spurned his attentions then begin their last ride together.

The effect on the narrator of the exhilarating moment which has preceded the ride is, through the very act of riding itself, sustained, and he begins to think of the ride as a perpetuation of their union. Thus he feels that he is superior to the poet, who can only describe what lovers feel,

> What does it all mean, poet? well,
> Your brain's [*sic*] beat into rhythm—you tell
> What we felt only;
>
> (I, 188)

to the sculptor, who makes a Venus of his art,

> And you, great sculptor—so you gave
> A score of years to art, her slave,
> And that's your Venus;
>
> (I, 189)

and to the musician, who can communicate nothing,

> What, man of music, you, grown grey
> With notes and nothing else to say.
>
> (I, 189)

But the speaker is not very realistic: he is unwilling to face the termination of the ride, which will efface the lingering grasp he still has on his "infinite moment"; and he wishes that the ride could continue forever so that "the instant" could be "made eternity" (I, 190). We are given an indication of the isolation he will feel when he and his lover are finally separated in "Two in the Campagna," which describes the painful awareness of a man who has experienced the "good minute," but has been unable to extend it.

Like the narrator in "The Last Ride Together," the speaker in "Two in the Campagna" has, through an instant of physical contact, known what love can mean:

> I kiss your cheek,
> Catch your soul's warmth,—I pluck the rose
> And love it more than tongue can speak—
> Then the good minute goes.               (II, 208)

But because his companion cannot give herself completely to the union he so ardently desires—"I would that you were all to me, / You that are just so much, no more" (II, 207)—the "minute" quickly slips away—"Already how am I so far / Out of that minute?"—and he realizes that "Fixed by no friendly star" he must, like the thistle ball, roll on "whenever light winds blow" (II, 208). Having tasted the fruits of love, ever so fleetingly, has allowed him to perceive the chasm which exists between the fulfillment of love and its privation:

> Where is the thread now? Off again!
> The old trick! Only I discern—
> Infinite passion and the pain
> Of finite hearts that yearn.               (II, 209)

The final stage in the descending scale of love experiences in *Men and Women* is examined in "A Serenade at the Villa." In this poem we are given a description of the complete negation of love which contrasts both in mood and meaning with "One Word More," "By the Fireside," and "Love Among the Ruins."[5] Each of the speakers in

[5] "The Statue and the Bust" also treats a failure to grasp love, but in this case Browning is using the love situation to explore a more complex matter—the withdrawal of the lovers from the moral struggle of life. See W. O. Raymond's penetrating analysis, "Browning's 'Statue and the Bust,'" in *The Infinite Moment and Other Essays in Robert Browning* (2d ed.; Toronto: University of Toronto Press, 1965), pp. 214–233.

these poems, and Browning, has found his "moon," the "guiding star" that eludes the aspiring lover in "Two in the Campagna." "A Serenade" is without love, and therefore without light:

> That was I, you heard last night
> When there rose no moon at all,
> Nor, to pierce the strained and tight
> Tent of heaven, a planet small:
> Life was dead, and so was light.
>
> (I, 117)

The poem creates a mood of lifelessness which, for Browning, is the inevitable result of unrequited love. Even the earth protests the oppression of the night—"Earth turned in her sleep with pain" (I, 118) —and when a light does appear in a flash from the sky, it results in a few drops of rain which, rather than alleviate the heaviness of the atmosphere, only serve to intensify the lover's hopelessness:

> In at heaven and out again,
> Lightning!—where it broke the roof,
> Bloodlike, some few drops of rain.
>
> (I, 118)

Finally, after bidding his mistress view his song and his attempt at fulfillment with favor, the narrator ends his lament with the declaration that, to add to his futility, he even finds the environment itself threatening:

> Oh, how dark your villa was,
> Windows fast and obdurate!
> How the garden grudged me grass
> Where I stood—the iron gate
> Ground its teeth to let me pass!
>
> (I, 121)

Although Browning does treat this situation rather humorously by placing an exaggerated emphasis on the narrator's difficulties, this same exaggeration, in its grimness, points to the importance for Browning of love's realization.

The viewpoint expressed in all of these poems is derived from Browning's treatment of love in his earlier poetry, and from his personal experience with Elizabeth Barrett Browning. Love's superiority, the potentially beneficial influence of the woman, and the necessity of a successful love union are all ideas which have as their source the theory that love is the "basis of the plan" of salvation. In *Men and Women* Browning utilizes these ideas as well as the symbolism with which they are associated, particularly in *Sordello*, to consider human love from various angles. By dealing with complete, partial, and negated love, the poet effectively examines thematic possibilities which are inherent in the theory of human love he had developed up to *Christmas-Eve and Easter-Day*.

Browning's career was devoted to finding the means which would enable him to attain that limited degree of "absolute vision" accessible to man. He gradually learned in *Paracelsus* and *Sordello* that the only way to accomplish this is by working through the real, or the physical. In *Men and Women*, he celebrates love as the power which allows man to use flesh as a medium through which that "vision" can be realized. Some lovers fail in attaining this movement to higher values either because their love experience is thwarted, as in "A Serenade at the Villa," or because they can triumph only momentarily over the grinding mortal power which oppresses love, as in "Two in the Campagna" and "The Last Ride Together." Others, such as those in "One Word More," "By the Fireside," and "Love Among the Ruins," succeed because they understand the obstructions which face them, but they also realize that in their imperfection created things can serve as instruments which ultimately lead, through human love, to a fuller appreciation of spiritual perfection.

### OF RELIGION

"An Epistle Containing the Strange Medical Experience of Karshish, the Arab Physician" and "Cleon" are poems based on the Incarnation. As such, they are clearly the result of Browning's personal meditations in *Christmas-Eve and Easter-Day*. Because he had accepted the Incarnation as the most important doctrine of his own religious creed, Browning was able, in these two poems, to examine with a considerable degree of objectivity the significance of the coming of Christ as a historical event. Through the characterizations of an Arab physician and a highly gifted Greek philosopher, Browning depicts the impact which the Incarnation might have had on those who were allowed to experience it as a contemporary event. But although "Karshish" and "Cleon" are objective in the sense that they are devoted to the revelation of highly individualized characters in particular circumstances at a specific point in time, and although they may be said to contain no "argument,"[6] they do reveal the particular bias of Browning's religious thought in 1855—the importance of a belief in the incarnated Christ as representative of the intimate connection which exists between the temporal and the eternal. For Karshish, healthy curiosity leaves open the possibility of eventual acceptance. For Cleon, intellectual pride is an obstacle which closes his mind to the acceptance of what he so desperately requires.

Karshish, "the picker-up of learning's crumbs" (I, 90), is reporting the progress of his travels to his medical and academic superior Abib in a letter. Wearied by his long and difficult journey from Jericho to Bethany, yet eager to share with his chief "whatever Jewry yields" (I, 92), he records his thoughts haphazardly, as they come to him. He reports that a Roman invasion seems imminent, and that in the course of his journey he encountered a lynx, was twice beaten and robbed, and in one town was accused of being a spy. Then he turns to medical matters, offering his observations on the condition of choler, falling sickness, scalp disease, and leprosy in the Jewish state. But his descent to the mention of such a trivial matter as the superior quality of Judea's gum tragacanth, combined with such cursory medical opinions, reminds him of the original purpose he had in writing the letter—to describe a strange medical phenomenon that he is rather embarrassed to admit has caught his attention—"I half resolve to tell thee, yet I blush, / What set me off a-writing first of all" (I, 93).

Karshish has come upon the very strange case of a man named Lazarus who, after being in a trance for three days, was cured by some medical means unknown to Arab science. Although this man thinks he died and was then restored to life "By a Nazarene physician of his tribe" (I, 95), this is, according to Karshish, clearly a "case of mania—subinduced / By epilepsy" (I, 94). But, he adds, imagine what a contribution to medicine it would be to discover the physician's secret. The patient Lazarus appears to be in sound physical health:

[6] See H. B. Charlton's analysis in his "Browning as a Poet of Religion," *Bulletin of John Rylands Library*, XXVII (1942–1943), 271–307. See also William Irvine, "Four Monologues in Browning's *Men and Women*," *Victorian Poetry*, II (Summer 1964), 160–163; and Wilfred L. Guerin, "Irony and Tension in Browning's 'Karshish,'" *Victorian Poetry*, I (April 1963), 132–139.

> Think, could we penetrate by any drug
> And bathe the wearied soul and worried flesh,
> And bring it clear and fair, by three days' sleep!
>
> (I, 96)

There is, however, one aspect of the cure which wholly mystifies Karshish. Lazarus is completely oblivious of things that are happening around him. He is, like a child, totally uninvolved in the problems of everyday adult life. Perhaps he is mad, for he appears to be in a "stupor," and yet the Arab has received the distinct impression that this man has somehow obtained a treasure denied to other human beings:

> we'll call the treasure knowledge, say—
> Increased beyond the fleshly faculty—
> Heaven opened to a soul while yet on earth,
> Earth forced on a soul's use while seeing Heaven.
>
> (I, 97)

Existing in two spheres at once, "His heart and brain move there, his feet stay here" (I, 99), Lazarus has explained that he is content to wait patiently for death,

> which will restore his being
> To equilibrium, body loosening soul
> Divorced even now by premature full growth.
>
> (I, 100–101)

Browning here again reverts to an important theme which runs through his earlier work. Although the cause of their problems is different, Sordello and Lazarus both suffer from a disharmony between soul and body. Lazarus, in his "stupor," is a practical demonstration of the idea expressed in *Pauline, Paracelsus*, and the *Essay on Shelley* that a total "absolute vision" is not for this world. Man, as man, cannot live in infinity.[7]

---

[7] See also "Bishop Blougram's Apology" (I, 239–240):

> Some think, Creation's meant to show him forth:
> I say, it's meant to hide him all it can,
> And that's what all the blessed Evil's for.
> Its use in time is to environ us,
> Our breath, our drop of dew, with shield enough
> Against that sight till we can bear its stress.

Despite his attempt to retain his status as an aloof medical observer, Karshish has been unable to remain uninvolved in a matter which so excites his curiosity. He would have contacted "the learned leech" (I, 103), but unfortunately he has suffered the common fate of medical men and been put to death for wizardry some years before. And here lies the strangest part of the whole affair. Several miraculous events have been attributed to this Jewish physician, but Lazarus, who must be "stark mad" (I, 103), goes so far as to believe that the "leech" was God Himself in human form:

> This man so cured regards the curer then,
> As—God forgive me—who but God himself,
> Creator and Sustainer of the world,
> That came and dwelt in flesh on it awhile!
>
> (I, 104)

Enough of this matter, exclaims Karshish. He apologizes that he is tired and has lost all sense of the relative importance of things. A trained observer should not become a superstitious gossip. But even after formally closing the letter, Karshish cannot help but speculate on the possibility that perhaps there may be some truth in all of this:

> The very God! think, Abib; dost thou think?
> So, the All-Great, were the All-Loving too—
> So, through the thunder comes a human voice
> Saying, "O heart I made, a heart beats here!
> Face, my hands fashioned, see it in myself.
> Thou hast no power nor may'st conceive of mine,
> But love I gave thee, with Myself to love,
> And thou must love me who have died for thee!"
> The madman saith He said so: it is strange.
>
> (I, 105–106)

"Karshish" is a masterful presentation on Browning's part of the processes of a mind goaded on to investigation by skeptical curiosity. And Karshish is by no means a static figure. After following the Arab physician's progress from outright incredulity to wondering half-belief, the reader is left with the impression that Karshish is only one

---

Under a vertical sun, the exposed brain
And lidless eye and disemprisoned heart
Less certainly would wither up at once
Than mind, confronted with the truth of Him.

step away from the personal application of his discovery of the immensity of Divine love and its consequence in the Incarnation. In contrast, Cleon is not so fortunate.

Cleon thinks too much, and, as Browning shows in *Christmas-Eve and Easter-Day*, too great a reliance on rationality is a dangerous thing. With his highly trained intellect, Cleon has delved into the fundamental problems of existence and discovered the answer to the contradiction posed by the theory of progress which, for the non-Christian, can only end with the recession into death. His answer is that there is no answer. The poem is an elucidation, again in epistolary form, of the process through which he has arrived at this negation, and his resultant blindness to the Incarnation, which holds the only possible solution to his philosophic queries.

Cleon's letter is written in response to the Greek king Protus' plea for advice. Protus fears that the end of life will, for him, be the end of existence, and he sees in the many accomplishments of Cleon one means by which man can live on after death. He asks Cleon how he too might gain some measure of immortality.

While he admits that he is an example of perfection according to the natural law of progress, that in combining the "perfect separate forms" of poetry, music, painting, and philosophy into "the combination of the same" (II, 176), he has achieved the most that man can, Cleon knows that there is a disparity between the theory of natural perfection and his own unsatisfying experience. Ideally, man's life is an ordered progression in the growth of consciousness. This is what separates him from the animal; and, at least theoretically, the more he learns of his powers the happier he will be:

> Man might live at first
> The animal life: but is there nothing more?
> In due time, let him critically learn
> How he lives; and, the more he gets to know
> Of his own life's adaptabilities,
> The more joy-giving will his life become.
>
> (II, 182)

However, Cleon admits that in reality the pessimistic philosophy of King Protus is closer to the truth. "Most progress is most failure" (II, 185) because as man advances in self-consciousness he learns that there is a world of joy, of realization of soul, that he can never fully experience. Man can always attempt to enlarge his capacity, but, as Browning illustrated in the case of Sordello, he is doomed to failure, without hope of ever bridging the gap between what he knows he can be and what he is. In Protus' mind, Cleon is a possible exception. Because he possesses "artist's gifts," complete joy may be possible to him, and he at least will survive after death through his works. But Cleon points out that his case is even more pitiable than those men who possess a less refined sensitivity. There is, he explains, a great difference between describing joy and experiencing it, between showing others how to live and knowing how to live oneself, between painting and acting. Because he knows what is best, he can understand more fully than others how he himself fails in attaining it:

> Say rather that my fate is deadlier still,—
> In this, that every day my sense of joy
> Grows more acute, my soul (intensified
> In power and insight) more enlarged, more keen;
> While every day my hairs fall more and more,
> My hand shakes, and the heavy years increase—
> The horror quickening still from year to year,
> The consummation coming past escape.          (II, 187)

Like Protus, Cleon will die. His works will only serve to mock him in death, not to grant him immortality.

The prospect of such finality is so horrifying to Cleon that he admits he has even allowed himself to imagine that Zeus has revealed a state of perpetual life after death, in which all the problems of temporality and unrealized fulfillment would be resolved:

> I dare at times imagine to my need
> Some future state revealed to us by Zeus,
> Unlimited in capability
> For joy, as this is in desire for joy,
> To seek which, the joy-hunger forces us.
> That, stung by straitness of our life, made strait
> On purpose to make sweet the life at large—
> Freed by the throbbing impulse we call death
> We burst there as the worm into the fly,
> Who, while a worm still, wants his wings.          (II, 188)

However, Zeus has not yet supplied this comfort, and it is Cleon's intellectual conviction that he would have done so "were it possible" (II, 188). The artist in Cleon has, through imaginative speculation, led him to the threshold of truth, but the philosopher in Cleon rejects its possibility, just as he scornfully dismisses the absurd notion that "Paulus" or "Christus," "a mere barbarian Jew" (II, 189), could have "access to a secret" denied to the most highly developed Greek mind. By decisively rejecting the answer he seeks on the grounds that "Their doctrines could be held by no sane man" (II, 189), Cleon's intellect defeats itself.

Browning's analysis of an Arab physician's and a Greek philosopher's reactions to Christianity illustrates more than the poet's particular view of the receptivity of the Arab and Greek cultures, which these men represent, to Christianity. Through his apparently detached examination of particular characters, Browning is again stating a case for Christianity which reflects his own personal convictions. In the figure of Christ, the God-man, the Divinity who partakes of the mundane, man finds the solution to the riddle of his own paradoxical quest: it is the union of the spotted and the pure, not their separation, which enables man to truly fulfill his potential.

## OF ART

David's success as a poet in "Saul" establishes a standard of judgment through which Browning evaluates the success or failure of the various artist figures in *Men and Women*. Reduced to its simplest terms, Browning's theory of art, as summarized in the *Essay on Shelley* and worked out in "Saul," is that the "whole poet" has the ability to integrate the roles of the fashioner and the seer. Thus, while discounting the artist's power to encompass an "absolute vision" in his work, Browning contends that a true artist does bring into harmony the "raw material" of reality, which is the proper sphere of the fashioner, and the "spiritual comprehension" of the seer. Unity through the fusion of dualities is the cental principle of Browning's mature aesthetic theory, and it is the struggle to understand how this unity can be achieved which is the predominant motif of the poetry written during the period of his development from 1833 to 1851. "Saul" and the other art poems in *Men and Women* indicate that by 1855 Browning was no longer searching for an answer to this fundamental theoretical problem.

Fra Lippo Lippi is the David of painters, and perhaps even more explicitly than David, he serves as a mouthpiece for Browning's ideas on the nature of art. He is a prime example of the "whole" artist, whose function, as stated in the *Essay on Shelley*, is to behold "with an understanding keenness the universe, nature and man, in their actual state of perfection in imperfection." However, this artist-monk is ruled by superiors who have, in their devotion to the spiritual values which it is their vocation to promulgate, forgotten that man is, after all, made of flesh and blood, as well as soul.

When asked by his prior to apply his artistic ability to church decoration, Fra Lippo Lippi follows his natural inclination and paints with such realistic accuracy that his brother monks are able to identify in the mural specific individuals from the church congregation. The prior is not at all pleased; to him, the purpose of art is to offer spiritual inspiration, not to glorify the body:

> it's devil's-game!
> Your business is not to catch men with show,
> With homage to the perishable clay,
> But lift them over it, ignore it all,
> Make them forget there's such a thing as flesh.
> Your business is to paint the souls of men.
>
> (I, 44)

However, despite his conviction of what art must do, the monastic superior is not quite so certain how one goes about depicting such an "absolute vision" as man's soul:

> Man's soul, and it's a fire, smoke . . no it's not . .
> It's vapour done up like a new-born babe—
> (In that shape when you die it leaves your mouth)
> It's . . well, what matters talking, it's the soul!
>
> (I, 44)

Fra Lippo Lippi knows that this view of art is invalid. His purpose in painting is not to glorify the flesh, but to employ it as a means through which man can more easily perceive soul. The "raw material" of art, in Browning's terminology, is the "starting point" which can lead to greater "spiritual comprehension":

> Why can't a painter lift each foot in turn,
> Left foot and right foot, go a double-step,

> Make his flesh liker and his soul more like,
> Both in their order?
>
> . . . . . . . . . . .
>
> Can't I take breath and try to add life's flash,
> And then add soul and heighten them threefold?
>
> (I, 45–46) [8]

To justify this concept, which is clearly derived from Browning's understanding of the Incarnation and the flesh-spirit synthesis in "Saul," Fra Lippo places his theory in a thoroughly Christian context. He believes only what he has been taught—that the flesh is good:

> For me, I think I speak as I was taught—
> I always see the Garden and God there
> A-making man's wife—and, my lesson learned,
> The value and significance of flesh,
> I can't unlearn ten minutes afterwards.
>
> (I, 48–49)

And from the flesh he moves to a defense of the beauty that shines through the imperfection of all created things. He sees, like Aprile in *Paracelsus* and the narrator of *Easter-Day*, that the beauty of the world, the "weeds" of existence, have value because they are created by God and reflect, however minutely, His glory:

> —The beauty and the wonder and the power,
> The shapes of things, their colours, lights and shades,
> Changes, surprises,—and God made it all!
>
> (I, 49)

Fra Lippo's superiors, like Paracelsus and Sordello, would neglect the finite in their effort to reach the infinite. But the monk understands the futility of such endeavors. By dealing with the actual, art does not limit man's vision; rather, it allows him to perceive beauty of which he had hitherto been unaware, to see meaning in the commonplace:

[8] The terms of conflict in "Fra Lippo Lippi" are exactly parallel to those employed in "Old Pictures in Florence." Greek art presented an ideal: "So you saw yourself as you wished you were, / As you might have been, as you cannot be" (II, 36); but early Christian art was superior because, concentrating on man "rough-hewn, no-wise polished" (II, 38), it led him to an understanding of his own nobility: "What if we so small / Are greater, ay, greater the while than they" (II, 37).

> we're made so that we love
> First when we see them painted, things we have passed
> Perhaps a hundred times nor cared to see;
> And so they are better, painted—better to us,
> Which is the same thing. Art was given for that—
> God uses us to help each other so,
> Lending our minds out.
>
> (I, 50)

For Browning and Fra Lippo Lippi, the artist becomes a communicator who must apprehend the significance of reality.[9] He cannot depict soul alone: he must orient his vision to a sphere that allows him to take cognizance of the limitations of his own capabilities and those of his fellow man:

> This world's no blot for us,
> Nor blank—it means intensely, and means good:
> To find its meaning is my meat and drink.
>
> (I, 51)

While David and Fra Lippo Lippi successfully fulfill Browning's view of art because their work achieves meaning through the fusion of the flesh and the spirit, the real and the ideal, Andrea del Sarto and Master Hughes of Saxe-Gotha are Browning's contrasting examples of the extremes of artistic failure. Andrea is the "Faultless Painter" whose work presents a perfect pictorial image of flesh but has no soul. Master Hughes, a musician, produces only abstract, intellectual fugues, and thus his music lacks flesh. Because the work of each of these men is deficient in one of the two areas demanded by Browning for successful art, neither of them can capture meaning.

Andrea del Sarto's artistic deficiency is illustrated by his inability to correct a flaw in a painting by Rafael. He recognizes that although Rafael's drawing is technically imperfect, his work does nevertheless allow the soul to shine through:

> That arm is wrongly put—and there again—
> A fault to pardon in the drawing's lines,
> Its body, so to speak! its soul is right.
>
> (II, 7)

[9] Cf. W. David Shaw, "Character and Philosophy in 'Fra Lippo Lippi,'" *Victorian Poetry*, II (Spring 1964), 127–132.

But Andrea, fully aware of his own talent as a draftsman—"No sketches first, no studies, that's long past—/ I do what many dream of all their lives" (II, 4)—cannot tolerate such a flaw. He attempts to alter Rafael's work, and in doing so only succeeds in destroying its essential quality, its soul:

> And indeed the arm is wrong.
> I hardly dare—yet, only you to see,
> Give the chalk here—quick, thus the line should go!
> Ay, but the soul! he's Rafael! rub it out!
>
> (II, 11)

"Andrea del Sarto" is, however, more than just another statement by Browning on the necessity of integrating flesh and soul to achieve meaning. Of equal interest is the poet's comment on the cause of Andrea's failure—his complete devotion to a woman who has proven herself to be a negative source of inspiration. Andrea describes his wife Lucrezia in language which recalls the significance Browning attaches to the potentially beneficial influence of a woman in *Sordello* and "One Word More." Lucrezia is his moon, but she is also everyone else's: "My face, my moon, my everybody's moon" (II, 2). The artist's painting, for which Lucrezia always serves as a model, exactly parallels in its strength and its weakness the physical beauty and spiritual emptiness of his wife:

> all the play, the insight and the stretch—
> Out of me! out of me! And wherefore out?
> Had you enjoined them on me, given me soul,
> We might have risen to Rafael, I and you.
>
> . . . . . . . . . .
>
> had you—oh, with the same perfect brow,
> And perfect eyes, and more than perfect mouth,
>
> . . . . . . . . . . . .
>
> Had you, with these the same, but brought a mind!
>
> (II, 7)

And even though he understands the cause of his failure—"One picture, just one more—the Virgin's face, / Not your's this time" (II, 12–13)—Andrea, bound by the very flesh which is his nemesis to his negative moon, will never be able to rise above the mere depiction of perfect but earth-bound beauty.

Master Hughes of Saxe-Gotha is, on the other hand, so involved

with the intellectual perfection of musical composition that he completely ignores the necessity of effecting the marriage of the concrete
and the abstract.[10] Although there is a similarity between Andrea and
Master Hughes in that they are both technicians of considerable ability,
the two men differ in the ways they fail because of a difference in the
mediums with which they work. In the pictorial art of Andrea, significance is strictly limited to the literal physical image he creates on
canvas. In the music of Hughes of Saxe-Gotha, mastery of the difficult
fugal structure indicates that the composer has risen above Andrea's
physical sphere, but such an achievement is equally worthless, because,
like the spider web that hides the gilt roof of the church in which the
fugue is being played—"See our roof, its gilt moulding and groining /
Under those spider-webs lying!" (I, 200)—it can offer only an empty
answer to the problems of temporal existence:

> Is it your moral of Life?
> Such a web, simple and subtle,
> Weave we on earth here in impotent strife,
> Backward and forward each throwing his shuttle,
> Death ending all with a knife?
>
> (I, 201)

Moreover, the fugue of Master Hughes is no more helpful as a guide to
understanding that which lies beyond temporality. Again, like the
spider web that obscures the roof, the composer's music only serves to
blot out the golden truth of Heaven:

> not a glimpse of the far land
> Gets through our comments and glozes.
>
> . . . . . . . . . .
>
> Truth's golden o'er us although we refuse it—
> Nature, thro' dust-clouds we fling her!
>
> (I, 202–203)

Browning admits in *Sordello*, *Easter-Day*, the *Essay on Shelley* and
"One Word More" that art will always be inadequate, but the music
of Master Hughes is more than inadequate: it is a dense dust cloud

---

[10] Cf. Richard D. Altick, "The Symbolism of Browning's 'Master Hughes of
Saxe-Gotha,'" *Victorian Poetry*, III (Winter 1965), 1–7; and George M. Ridenour,
"Browning's Music Poems: Fancy and Fact," *PMLA*, LXXVIII (September
1963), 375.

obscuring even the slightest gleam which radiates from the golden truth that lies beyond the finite. Thus, the "poor organist," who serves as the narrator of the poem, is prompted to ask the inevitable Browning question—what is any art worth that means nothing, either because it dwells on the concrete as in Andrea's case, or is devoted solely to abstract intellectual creation as in the music of Master Hughes:

> Forth and be judged, Master Hughes!
> Answer the question I've put you so oft—
> What do you mean by your mountainous fugues?

> (I, 194)

Browning's question is, of course, a rhetorical one. Any art, whether it be music, sculpture, painting, or poetry, is worth little to Browning unless it is, as he wrote in a letter to Ruskin in 1855, "a putting the infinite within the finite."[11] And this clearly is both what Browning thinks art must do, and what he himself does in his own best poetry. Through his thematic treatment of love, religion, and art in *Men and Women*, the poet is simultaneously stating a theory and practicing it himself. By treating men and women, by devoting his full energy to the depiction of character, Browning uses the "flesh" to help illuminate the "soul." And the theory in *Men and Women*, based on the three areas of human endeavor which Browning had been experiencing and examining in purely personal terms up to 1851, and which as a whole is most accurately described as a moral-aesthetic philosophy, is the culmination of two decades of frustrating and frequently unrewarding poetry, both for Browning and for his readers.

Browning's long period of painful self-scrutiny, beginning in 1833 and extending to the *Essay on Shelley* in 1851, did finally bear fruit. The "palm wine" of *Men and Women*, and later of *Dramatis Personae* and *The Ring and the Book*, which is the result of the "palm's self . . . slow growth"—evidenced by the poetry of the 1830's and 1840's—is perhaps the most fitting illustration of Browning's own theoretical principle that the limited perfection of which man is capable grows out of the imperfection in which he finds himself initially, and necessarily, involved. But here the analogy ends. Although Browning proclaims in "Saul" that "stem and branch / Shall decay, nor be known in their

[11] Quoted by E. T. Cook in *The Life of John Ruskin* (London: G. Allen, 1912), I, 461.

place," a study of Browning's poetry reveals that it is only by under-standing the place, and the function, of the stem and branch that the flavor of the resultant full-bodied wine can be wholly appreciated.

# Selected Bibliography

WORKS OF BROWNING (Arranged chronologically)

*Pauline: The Text of 1833, Compared With That of 1867 and 1888,* ed. N. Hardy Wallis. London: University of London Press, 1931.

"Eyes Calm Beside Thee," *Monthly Repository,* N.S. VIII (October 1834), 712.

*Paracelsus.* London, 1835.

"A King Lived Long Ago," *Monthly Repository,* N.S. IX (November 1835), 707–708.

"Johannes Agricola," *Monthly Repository,* X (January 1836), 45–46.

"Porphyria," *Monthly Repository,* X (January 1836), 43–44.

"Still Ailing, Wind? Wilt Be Appeased or No?" *Monthly Repository,* N.S. X (May 1836), 270–271.

*Strafford: An Historical Tragedy.* London, 1837.

*Sordello.* London, 1840.

*Bells and Pomegranates. No. I.—Pippa Passes.* London, 1841.

*Bells and Pomegranates. No. II.—King Victor and King Charles.* London, 1842.

*Bells and Pomegranates. No. III.—Dramatic Lyrics.* London, 1842.

*Bells and Pomegranates. No. IV.—The Return of the Druses.* London, 1843.

*Bells and Pomegranates. No. V.—A Blot in the 'Scutcheon.* London, 1843.

*Bells and Pomegranates. No. VI.—Colombe's Birthday.* London, 1844.

*Bells and Pomegranates. No. VII.—Dramatic Romances and Lyrics.* London, 1845.

*Bells and Pomegranates. No. VIII.—And Last. Luria: And A Soul's Tragedy.* London, 1846.

*Christmas-Eve and Easter-Day.* London, 1850.

"An Essay on Shelley" (1852). In *The Complete Poetical Works of Robert Browning*, ed. Horace E. Scudder. Cambridge ed. Boston, 1895.

*Men and Women*. 2 vols. London, 1855.

*The Works of Robert Browning*, ed. F. G. Kenyon. 10 vols. London: Smith, Elder, 1912.

*New Poems by Robert Browning and Elizabeth Barrett Browning*, ed. F. G. Kenyon. London: Smith, Elder, 1914.

### BIOGRAPHY AND CRITICISM

ALTICK, RICHARD D. "Browning's 'Transcendentalism,'" *JEGP*, LVIII (1959), 24–28.

———. "The Private Life of Robert Browning," *Yale Review*, XLI (1951), 247–262.

———. "The Symbolism of Browning's 'Master Hughes of Saxe-Gotha,'" *Victorian Poetry*, III (Winter 1965), 1–7.

BADGER, KINGSBURY. "'See the Christ Stand!': Browning's Religion," *Boston University Studies in English*, I (1955), 53–73.

BENHAM, A. R. "Shelley and Browning," *Modern Language Notes*, XXXVIII (December 1923), 503.

BOAS, F. S. "Robert Browning's 'Paracelsus,' 1835–1935," *Quarterly Review*, CCLXV (October 1935), 280–295.

BROOKE, STOPFORD A. *The Poetry of Robert Browning*. London: Isbister, 1902.

BROUGHTON, L. N., C. S. NORTHUP, AND R. PEARSALL. *Robert Browning: A Bibliography, 1830–1950*. Ithaca: Cornell University Press, 1953.

BROWNING, ELIZABETH BARRETT. *The Letters of Elizabeth Barrett Browning*, ed. F. G. Kenyon. 2 vols. London, 1897.

BROWNING, ROBERT. *The Letters of Robert Browning and Elizabeth Barrett Barrett, 1845–1846*. 2 vols. London, 1899.

———. *Letters of Robert Browning, Collected by Thomas J. Wise*, ed. Thurman L. Hood. New Haven: Yale University Press, 1933.

———. *New Letters of Robert Browning*, ed. W. C. DeVane and Kenneth L. Knickerbocker. New Haven: Yale University Press, 1950.

———. *Robert Browning and Alfred Domett*, ed. F. G. Kenyon. London: Smith, Elder, 1906.

CHARLTON, H. B. "Browning as Dramatist," *Bulletin of John Rylands Library*, XXIII (1939), 33–67.

———. "Browning's Ethical Poetry," *Bulletin of John Rylands Library*, XXVII (1942–1943), 36–69.

———. "Browning As Poet of Religion," *Bulletin of John Rylands Library*, XXVII (1942–1943), 271–307.

———. "The Making of the Dramatic Lyric," *Bulletin of John Rylands Library*, XXXV (1952–1953), 349–384.

COLUMBUS, R. R., AND C. KEMPER. "Sordello and the Speaker: A Problem in Identity," *Victorian Poetry*, II (Autumn 1964), 251–267.

COOK, E. T. *The Life of John Ruskin.* 2 vols. London: G. Allen, 1912.

CRAMER, MAURICE B. "Browning's Friendships and Fame Before Marriage (1833–1846)," *PMLA*, LV (1940), 207–230.

CRAWFORD, A. W. "Browning's *Christmas-Eve*," *Methodist Review*, CX (May 1927), 379–382.

———. "Browning's 'Saul,'" *Queen's Quarterly*, XXXIV (1927), 448–454.

CROWELL, NORTON B. *The Triple Soul: Browning's Theory of Knowledge.* Albuquerque: University of New Mexico Press, 1963.

CUNLIFFE, J. W. "Elizabeth Barrett's Influence on Browning's Poetry," *PMLA*, XXIII (June 1908), 169–183.

[CUNNINGHAM, A.] Review of *Pauline*, *Athenaeum* (April 6, 1833), p. 216.

DEVANE, WILLIAM C. *A Browning Handbook.* 2d ed. New York: Appleton-Century-Crofts, 1955. First ed., 1935.

———. *Browning's Parleyings, The Autobiography of a Mind.* New Haven: Yale University Press, 1927.

———. "*Sordello's* Story Retold," *Studies in Philology*, XXVII (January 1930), 1–24.

DREW, PHILIP. "Browning's *Essay on Shelley*," *Victorian Poetry*, I (January 1963), 1–6.

DUBOIS, ARTHUR E. "Robert Browning, Dramatist," *Studies in Philology*, XXXIII (1936), 626–655.

DUCKWORTH, FRANCIS R. *Browning: Background and Conflict.* New York: E. P. Dutton, 1932.

FAIRCHILD, HOXIE N. "Browning the Simple Hearted Casuist," *University of Toronto Quarterly*, XVIII (April 1949), 234–240.

FAIRCHILD, HOXIE N. *Religious Trends in English Poetry*, IV, 1830–1880. New York: Columbia University Press, 1957.

[FORSTER, JOHN.] "Evidence of a New Genius For Dramatic Poetry: No. 1," *New Monthly Magazine and Literary Journal*, XLVI (March 1836), 289–308.

[———.] "Performance of Strafford," *The Examiner* (May 7, 1837), pp. 294–295.

FOX, BERNICE. "Revision In Browning's *Paracelsus*," *Modern Language Notes*, LV (March 1940), 195–197.

[FOX, W. J.] Review of *Pauline*, *Monthly Repository*, N.S. VII (April 1833), 252–262.

GLEN, MARGARET ELEANOR. "The Meaning and Structure of *Pippa Passes*," *University of Toronto Quarterly*, XXIV (1954–1955), 410–426.

GOSSE, EDMUND. *Robert Browning Personalia*. London, 1890.

GRIFFIN, W. H., AND H. C. MINCHIN. *The Life of Robert Browning*. New York: Macmillan, 1910.

GUERIN, WILFRED L. "Irony and Tension in Browning's 'Karshish,'" *Victorian Poetry*, I (April 1963), 132–139.

HAINES, LEWIS F. "Mill and *Pauline*: the 'Review' That 'Retarded Browning's Fame,'" *Modern Language Notes*, LXIX (June 1944), 410–412.

HERFORD, C. H. *Robert Browning*. New York: Dodd, Mead, 1905.

HILTON, EARL. "Browning's *Sordello* as a Study of the Will," *PMLA*, LXIX (December 1954), 1127–1134.

HOLMES, STEWART W. "Browning: Semantic Stutterer," *PMLA*, LX (March 1945), 231–255.

———. "Browning's *Sordello* and Jung: Browning's *Sordello* in the Light of Jung's Theory of Types," *PMLA*, LVI (September 1941), 758–796.

———. "The Sources of Browning's *Sordello*," *Studies in Philology*, XXXIV (July 1937), 467–496.

HONAN, PARK. *Browning's Characters: A Study in Poetic Technique*. New Haven: Yale University Press, 1961.

IRVINE, WILLIAM. "Four Monologues in Browning's *Men and Women*," *Victorian Poetry*, II (Summer 1964), 155–164.

JOHNSON, E. D. H. *The Alien Vision of Victorian Poetry*. Princeton: Princeton University Press, 1952.

JONES, HENRY. *Browning as a Philosophical and Religious Teacher.* New York, 1891.

KENMARE, DALLAS. *An End to Darkness.* London: P. Owen, 1962.

———. *Ever a Fighter.* London: John Barrie, 1952.

KING, ROMA A. *The Bow and the Lyre.* Ann Arbor: University of Michigan Press, 1957.

KNICKERBOCKER, KENNETH L. "A Tentative Apology for Browning," *Tennessee Studies in Literature,* I (1956), 75–82.

KRAMER, DALE. "Character and Theme in *Pippa Passes,*" *Victorian Poetry,* II (Autumn 1964), 241–249.

LANGBAUM, ROBERT. *The Poetry of Experience.* London: Chatto and Windus, 1957.

LITZINGER, BOYD. "Robert Browning and the Babylonian Women," *Baylor Browning Interests,* No. 19. Waco, 1962.

LOUNSBURY, THOMAS R. *The Early Literary Career of Robert Browning.* New York: Charles Scribner's Sons, 1911.

MACREADY, WILLIAM CHARLES. *The Diaries of William Charles Macready: 1833–1851,* ed. William Toynbee. 2 vols. London: Chapman and Hall, 1912.

MARTINEAU, HARRIET. *Autobiography,* ed. M. W. Chapman. 2 vols. Boston, 1877.

McPEEK, J. A. "The Shaping of 'Saul,'" *JEGP,* XLIV (October 1945), 360–366.

MILLER, BETTY. *Robert Browning: A Portrait.* New York: Charles Scribner's Sons, 1953.

MIYOSHI, MASAO. "Mill and 'Pauline': The Myth and Some Facts," *Victorian Studies,* IX (December 1965), 154–163.

Notice of *Pauline, The Literary Gazette* (March 23, 1833), p. 183.

Notice of *Pauline, Tait's Edinburgh Magazine,* III (August 1833), 668.

ORR, MRS. SUTHERLAND. *Life and Letters of Robert Browning.* 2 vols. Boston, 1891.

PHELPS, WILLIAM L. *Robert Browning.* 2d ed. Indianapolis: Bobbs-Merrill, 1932. First ed., 1915.

"The Poets of the Day: Batch the Third," *Fraser's Magazine,* XLVIII (December 1833), 658–670.

POTTLE, FREDERICK A. *Shelley and Browning: A Myth and Some Facts.* Chicago: Pembroke Press, 1923.

PREYER, ROBERT. "Robert Browning: A Reading of the Early

Narratives," *Journal of English Literary History*, XXVI (1959), 531–548.

PRIESTLEY, F. E. L. "The Ironic Pattern of Browning's *Paracelsus*," *University of Toronto Quarterly*, XXXIV (October 1964), 68–81.

RAYMOND, W. O. *The Infinite Moment and Other Essays in Robert Browning*. 2d ed. Toronto: University of Toronto Press, 1965. First ed., 1950.

Review of *A Blot in the 'Scutcheon*, *Athenaeum* (February 18, 1843), p. 166.

Review of *Paracelsus*, *Athenaeum* (August 2, 1835), p. 640.

Review of *Pauline*, *The Atlas* (April 14, 1833), p. 228.

RIDENOUR, GEORGE M. "Browning's Music Poems: Fancy and Fact," *PMLA*, LXXVIII (September 1963), 369–377.

RUSSELL, FRANCES T. *One Word More on Browning*. Stanford: Stanford University Press, 1927.

SHAW, W. D. "Character and Philosophy in 'Fra Lippo Lippi,'" *Victorian Poetry*, II (Spring 1964), 127–132.

———. "The Analogical Argument of Browning's 'Saul,'" *Victorian Poetry*, II (Autumn 1964), 277–282.

SMALLEY, DONALD. *Browning's Essay on Chatterton*. Cambridge, Massachusetts: Harvard University Press, 1948.

SMITH, C. WILLARD. *Browning's Star-Imagery*. Princeton: Princeton University Press, 1941.

SNYDER, EDWARD, AND FREDERIC PALMER. "New Light on the Brownings," *Quarterly Review*, CCLXIX (1937), 48–63.

STEMPEL, DANIEL. "Browning's *Sordello*: The Art of the Makers-See," *PMLA*, LXXX (December 1965), 554–561.

STEVENSON, LIONEL. *Darwin Among the Poets*. Chicago: University of Chicago Press, 1932.

———. "Tennyson, Browning, and a Romantic Fallacy," *University of Toronto Quarterly*, XIII (1944), 175–195.

THORPE, JAMES. "Elizabeth Barrett's Commentary on Shelley: Some Marginalia," *Modern Language Notes*, LXVI (1951), 455–458.

WALKER, HUGH. *The Greater Victorian Poets*. London, 1895.

WARREN, ALBA H. *English Poetic Theory, 1825–1865*. Princeton: Princeton University Press, 1950.

WENGER, CHRISTIAN N. *The Aesthetics of Robert Browning*. Ann Arbor: George Wahr, 1924.

WENGER, CHRISTIAN N. "The Masquerade in Browning's Dramatic Monologues," *College English*, III (1941), 225–239.

———. "Sources of Mill's Criticism of *Pauline*," *Modern Language Notes*, LX (1945), 338.

WHITLA, WILLIAM. *The Central Truth: The Incarnation in Robert Browning's Poetry*. Toronto: University of Toronto Press, 1963.

WILKINSON, D. C. "The Need for Disbelief: A Comment on *Pippa Passes*," *University of Toronto Quarterly*, XXIX (1959–1960), 139–151.


GENERAL STUDIES ON THE NINETEENTH CENTURY

ABRAMS, MEYER H. *The Mirror and the Lamp*. Norton Library ed. New York: W. W. Norton, 1958. First ed., 1953.

BRIGGS, ASA. *The Age of Improvement*. London: Longmans, Green, 1959.

BUCKLEY, JEROME. *The Victorian Temper*. Cambridge, Massachusetts: Harvard University Press, 1951.

BUSH, DOUGLAS. *Mythology and the Romantic Tradition In English Poetry*. Cambridge, Massachusetts: Harvard University Press, 1937.

*1859: Entering an Age of Crisis*. Ed. P. Appleman, W. Madden, and M. Wolff. Bloomington: Indiana University Press, 1959.

HALÉVY, ÉLIE. *England in 1815*. Trans. E. J. Watkins and D. A. Baker. 2d ed. London: Ernest Benn, 1960. First ed., 1924.

HEATH-STUBBS, JOHN. *The Darkling Plain*. London: Eyre and Spottis-woode, 1950.

HOLLOWAY, JOHN. *The Victorian Sage*. London: Macmillan, 1953.

HOUGHTON, WALTER E. *The Victorian Frame of Mind: 1830–1870*. New Haven: Yale University Press, 1957.

IRVINE, WILLIAM. *Apes, Angels, and Victorians*. New York: McGraw-Hill, 1955.

KITSON CLARK, G. *The Making of Victorian England*. London: Methuen, 1962.

MILLER, J. HILLIS. *The Disappearance of God*. Cambridge, Massachusetts: Harvard University Press, 1963.

PECKHAM, MORSE. *Beyond the Tragic Vision*. New York: George Braziller, 1962.

SOMERVELL, D. C. *English Thought in the Nineteenth Century*. London: Methuen, 1929.

WILLEY, BASIL. *More Nineteenth Century Studies*. London: Chatto and Windus, 1956.

————. *Nineteenth Century Studies*. London: Chatto and Windus, 1949.

WOODWARD, E. L. *The Age of Reform: 1815–1870*. 2d ed. Oxford: Clarendon Press, 1958. First ed., 1938.

YOUNG, G. M. *Victorian England: The Portrait of An Age*. 2d ed. London: Oxford University Press, 1953. First ed., 1936.

# Acknowledgments

I wish to express my gratitude to those who have helped to make this work possible. Donald J. Gray, Indiana University, sacrificed much of his time, and offered invaluable suggestions, throughout the preparation of the manuscript. Earle Sanborn, University of Western Ontario, first aroused my interest in Browning in his course on Victorian literature. Through the years he has been a teacher, an advisor, and a friend. Study grants from King's College, the Canada Council, and Indiana University are deeply appreciated. The Department of English, University of Western Ontario, generously supplied funds for proofreading and indexing.

The editors of *Victorian Poetry* have kindly allowed me to use material for this study which first appeared in the pages of their journal.

No expression of thanks to my wife would be adequate to compensate for the help she has given me.

THOMAS J. COLLINS

# Index

views on poet-philosopher, 94–95; avoided in *Pippa Passes*, 95; problem critical in *Saul*, 95; ideas traced through letters, 95; revisions in *Paracelsus*, 95–97; concept of love in *Paracelsus*, 97; liberal Christian survey, 99; attitude toward Roman Catholicism, 101–102; advanced and redefined, 112–113; influence of Elizabeth Barrett, 119–120, 129–130; theory reviewed, 121; *Saul* forms summary, 124; culmination of theory, 125; *Saul* forms link of Browning's ideas, 126; spiritual maturity, 131; values of love, 131–132; treatment of love summarized, 135–136; importance of Incarnation, 136; bias in religious thought, 137; position on Christianity, 142; theory of art, 142; Browning on art, 148n.; theory summarized, 148–149; *see also* Browning, Robert, *individual works*

*One Word More*, Elizabeth Barrett's influence, 128–129

Orr, Mrs. Sutherland, 9–10n.

*Paracelsus*, concentrates on moral ideas, 6; publication, 17n.; purpose, 17–18, 97; tone of preface, 18n.; Honan's views, 18–19n.; contrasted with *Pauline*, 19; achieves detachment, 19; Raymond's views, 19–20n.; DeVane's views, 20n.; Canto One, 20–25; setting and purpose, 20; value of love, 21; first indication of pride, 21; Festus' warnings, 21–23; seeks ultimate knowledge, 22–23; admiration of Michal, 23; Festus stresses human love, 23; conception of knowledge, 23–24; cause for failure, 24; Canto Two, 25–31; summary, 25; setting, 25; dejected from failure, 25–26; reflects on love, 26; changed idea of knowledge, 26–27; sea images, 27–28; learns of love and knowledge, 28; accepts God's will, 28; entrance of Aprile, 28; Raymond's views on Aprile, 28–29n.; theory regarding Aprile and Shelley, 29n.; Shelley-Browning relationship, 29–30; direction of poem, 30; Aprile converted from Shelleyism, 30; misinterprets Aprile, 30; rejects Aprile's pleas, 30–31; Canto Three, 31–34; new attitudes, 31; mocks Festus, 32; pride still uncontrolled, 32; dissatisfied at Basel, 32–33; recognizes his purpose, 33; admits past mistakes, 33; discouraged, 33; encouraged by Festus, 33–34; Festus as Browning's mouthpiece, 33–34; Browning's concept of love, 34; realizes his losses, 34; lacks

humility, 34; Canto Four, 34–37; appears as a drunken cynic, 34–35; outlines future courses, 35; new attitude, 35–36; lyrical parable, 36; aims reviewed, 36–37; blames failure on God, 37; Canto Five, 37–42; summary, 37–38; Festus seeks Paracelsus' salvation, 38; hierarchy of values, 38; Paracelsus and Aprile as Promethean figures, 38–39; withdrawal from human love reviewed, 39; attitude toward knowledge and man, 39–40; new understanding of dependency, 40–41; view of God, 40–41; new attitudes toward love and knowledge, 41; Browning's concerns, 41–42; poem's purpose compared to *Pauline*, 42; moral concerns, 42–43; solutions, 43; compared to *Sordello*, 45–46; explores moral questions, 45; achieves clarity, 46; compromise, 50; thematic development, 55; evolutionary theory, 57–58; reference to Christ, 94n.; revisions, 95–98; attitude toward God, 95–96; concept of love, Canto Five, 97; reconciles finite with infinite, 121; concept of love, 127

*Pauline*, Arnould's views, 3n.; DeVane's views, 3n.; compared to *Sartor Resartus* and *The Prelude*, 3–4; Mill's criticism, 4n.; basic structure, 4; poet's instability, 5n.; reviews Browning's life, 5; Browning's attitude toward Shelley, 5–6; praises Shelley, 7; Wallis' views, 7n.; recalls lost youth, 8; reveres Shelley, 8; unable to emulate Shelley, 8; purpose, 9; form, 9; mixed relationship with Shelley, 9; influence of ancient writings, 10; Browning leaves school, 10; poetic apprenticeship, 10–11; Byronic influence, 11n.; seeks freedom, 11; drawn to Shelley, 11–12; Browning dedicated to Shelley, 12; dream shattered, 12; optimism to pessimism, 12–13; last movement of poem, 13; religious affirmation, 13–14; Shelleyan devotion, 14; Miller's views, 14n.–15n.; resolution of poem, 15; thought pattern, 15; lack of clarity, 15; two poles of interest, 16; no defined ideas, 16; Browning's summation, 16n.; reviews, 17n.; tone of preface, 18n.; contrasted with *Paracelsus*, 19; compared to *Paracelsus*, 42; compared to *Sordello*, 45–46; contributes to structure of *Sordello*, 45; chaotic poem, 46; isolation theme, 50; reference to Christ, 94n.; poles of interest, 121; concept of love, 127

*Pippa Passes*, shows regression, 82, 92; poet figure's nature, 83; regression, 83; related

The central concern of Mr. Collins' study is the progressive development of Robert Browning's ideas on the nature and purpose of art, and on the role of the artist, between the years 1833 and 1855. While it has been generally recognized that the growth of Browning's aesthetic is closely related to his conception of man and of man's relationship to society, just as it is generally agreed that by 1855 Browning had clearly formulated his theory of imperfection, the present volume is the first single work to provide a detailed analysis of the development of Browning's moral-aesthetic ideas—the problems he faced, the solutions he formulated as he grew toward poetic maturity—and to scrutinize the intimate connection which exists between that mature work and the apprentice writing out of which it evolved.

Beginning with *Pauline* (1833), which is seen as a poem of irresolution, Mr. Collins takes up chronologically *Paracelsus* (1835), *Sordello* (1840), *Bells and Pomegranates* (1841–1846), revisions of *Paracelsus* (1849), *Christmas Eve and Easter-Day* (1850), the *Essay on Shelley* (1851), "Saul" (1845–1855), and finally *Men and Women* (1855), the work which represents the culmination of Browning's aesthetic development. This painstaking and perceptive examination of the long and difficult early works—so frequently ignored in the classroom—opens the way to a heightened appreciation of the mature writings, for they are the end-products of the decades of speculation and theoretical probing on which Mr. Collins has focused.

The clarity and organization of his analytical procedure will make this book a useful